First World War
and Army of Occupation
War Diary
France, Belgium and Germany

30 DIVISION
Divisional Troops
Divisional Ammunition Column
20 January 1914 - 11 December 1918

WO95/2321/8

The Naval & Military Press Ltd
www.nmarchive.com
Published in association with The National Archives

Published by

The Naval & Military Press Ltd

Unit 10 Ridgewood Industrial Park,

Uckfield, East Sussex,

TN22 5QE England

Tel: +44 (0) 1825 749494

www.naval-military-press.com

www.nmarchive.com

This diary has been reprinted in facsimile from the original. Any imperfections are inevitably reproduced and the quality may fall short of modern type and cartographic standards.

© **Crown Copyright**
Images reproduced by permission of The National Archives, London, England, 2015.

Contents

Document type	Place/Title	Date From	Date To
Heading	WO95/2321/8 30th Divl Ammn Column Sept 1915-Dec 1918		
Heading	30th Division Divl Artillery 30th Divl Ammn Column Sept 1915-Dec 1918		
Heading	30th Div 30th D.A.C. Vol: Dec 1915 Dec 1918		
Heading	War Diary Of 30th Divisional Ammunition Column From 25.8.15 To 31st December 1915 Volume I		
War Diary	St Ouen	06/12/1915	28/12/1915
War Diary	Grantham	28/08/1915	17/09/1915
War Diary	Larkhill	20/11/1915	28/11/1915
War Diary	Southampton	29/11/1915	29/11/1915
War Diary	Havre	30/11/1915	01/12/1915
War Diary	Doullens	02/12/1915	02/12/1915
War Diary	St Ouen	03/12/1915	05/12/1915
Heading	30th D.A.C. Vol: 2 Jan-16		
Heading	War Diary Of 30th Divisional Ammunition Column From 1.1.16 To 31.1.16 Volume 2		
War Diary	St Ouen	01/01/1916	19/01/1916
War Diary	Talmas	19/01/1916	19/01/1916
War Diary	Naours	19/01/1916	20/01/1916
War Diary	Pont Noyelles	20/01/1914	20/01/1914
War Diary	Lahoussoye	20/01/1914	20/01/1914
War Diary	Pont Noyelles	20/01/1916	20/01/1916
War Diary	Chipilly	21/01/1916	29/01/1916
Heading	30th Div A.C. Vol. 3		
Heading	War Diary Of 30th Divisional Ammunition Column J.P.D. Wheasley Lt. Col R.F.A. From 1st Feb 1916 To 28 Feb 1916 (Volume III)		
War Diary	Chipilly	01/02/1916	28/02/1916
War Diary	St Ouen		
War Diary	Week Ending	09/01/1916	30/01/1916
War Diary	Chipilly Week Ending	06/02/1916	27/02/1916
Heading	30 Div A. Col Vol 4		
Heading	War Diary Of 30th Divisional Ammunition Column Volume IV From 1st March 1916 To 31st March 1916		
War Diary	Chipilly	29/02/1916	23/03/1916
War Diary	Bussy	23/03/1916	27/03/1916
War Diary	Argoeuvres	27/03/1916	27/03/1916
War Diary	Ammunition issued March 1916	05/03/1916	26/03/1916
Heading	War Diary Of 30th Divisional Ammunition Column Volume 5 1st April 1916 30th April 1916		
War Diary	Argoeuvres	03/04/1916	21/04/1916
War Diary	Chipilly	24/04/1916	24/04/1916
War Diary	Argoeuvres	26/04/1916	26/04/1916
Miscellaneous	30th Div'nl. Arty No. 1462	14/05/1916	14/05/1916
Miscellaneous	O.B./818 General Staff, Fourth Army 163 (G).	06/05/1916	06/05/1916
Miscellaneous	Divisional Ammunition Column War Establishment		
Miscellaneous	Under the present system, the following personnel and vehicles are Employed in a Division for Ammunition supply. Figures approximate only.		

Miscellaneous	G.H.Q. No. O.B./818. Fourth Army No. 163 (G) XIII Corps No. Q.C. 1106. 30th Divn. O. 4888	26/05/1916	26/05/1916
Heading	War Diary Of 30 Divisional Ammunition Column Volume VI From 1st May 1916 To 31st May 1916		
War Diary	Argoeuvres	01/05/1916	05/05/1916
War Diary	Sailly Laurette	11/05/1916	18/05/1916
War Diary	Bray	18/05/1916	18/05/1916
War Diary	Chipilly	20/05/1916	23/05/1916
War Diary	Suzanne	20/05/1916	20/05/1916
War Diary	Sailly Laurette	22/05/1916	25/05/1916
War Diary	Week Ending	14/05/1916	28/05/1916
Miscellaneous	Officer i/c A.G's & Office Base.	23/07/1916	23/07/1916
Heading	War Diary of 30th Divisional Ammunition Column Volume VII From 1st June 1916 To 30th June 1916		
War Diary	Sailly Laurette	01/06/1916	01/06/1916
War Diary	Bois Des Tailles	03/06/1916	23/06/1916
War Diary	Sailly Laurette	23/06/1916	23/06/1916
War Diary	Week Ending	04/06/1916	25/06/1916
Heading	War Diary Of 30 Divisional Ammunition Column Volume VIII From 1.7.16 To 31.7.16		
War Diary	Sailly Laurette	10/07/1916	12/07/1916
War Diary	F.26.a.	18/07/1916	20/07/1916
War Diary	K.18.d.	20/07/1916	23/07/1916
Heading	30th Divisional Artillery 30th Divisional Ammunition Column R.F.A. August 1916		
War Diary	Bois Des Tailles	03/08/1916	03/08/1916
War Diary	Daours	05/08/1916	05/08/1916
War Diary	Tannay	06/08/1916	11/08/1916
War Diary	Bethune	19/08/1916	20/08/1916
War Diary		07/07/1916	29/08/1916
War Diary	Week Ending	06/08/1916	27/08/1916
Heading	War Diary Of 30th Divisional Ammunition Column For September 1916 Volume X		
War Diary	Bethune	09/09/1916	19/09/1916
War Diary	Monchy Cayeux	21/09/1916	21/09/1916
War Diary	Vacquerie	22/09/1916	22/09/1916
War Diary	Beauval	23/09/1916	23/09/1916
War Diary	Talmas	26/09/1916	26/09/1916
War Diary	Dernancourt	27/09/1916	27/09/1916
War Diary	Bethune	04/09/1916	31/09/1916
Heading	War Diary Of 30 Divisional Ammunition Column For October 1916 Volume XI		
War Diary	F.8.c.3.9	09/10/1916	11/10/1916
War Diary	S 26.C.	12/10/1916	21/10/1916
War Diary	Montauban	30/10/1916	30/10/1916
War Diary		28/10/1916	28/10/1916
War Diary	Week Ending	07/10/1916	31/10/1916
War Diary	Montauban	01/11/1916	18/11/1916
War Diary	Morlancourt	18/11/1916	18/11/1916
War Diary	Bonnay	19/11/1916	19/11/1916
War Diary	Talmas	20/11/1916	20/11/1916
War Diary	Milly	21/11/1916	24/11/1916
War Diary	Montauban	31/10/1916	31/10/1916
War Diary	Montauban	23/11/1916	23/11/1916
War Diary	Week Ending	07/11/1916	17/11/1916
War Diary	Saulty	02/12/1916	21/12/1916

Heading	War Diary Of 30th D.A.C. For January 1917 Volume 14 Dec 1918		
War Diary	Saulty	02/12/1916	13/01/1917
War Diary	Milly	13/01/1917	31/01/1917
War Diary		08/01/1917	29/01/1917
War Diary	Week Ending	07/01/1917	13/01/1917
Heading	War Diary Of 30th Divisional Ammunition Column For February 1917 Volume XV		
War Diary	Gouy En Artois		
War Diary	Week Ending	07/02/1917	28/02/1917
War Diary	Gouy-En-Artois	13/03/1917	16/03/1917
War Diary	Monchiet	16/03/1917	23/03/1917
War Diary	Gouy-En-Artois	12/03/1917	16/03/1917
War Diary	Monchiet	16/03/1917	31/03/1917
War Diary		03/03/1917	31/03/1917
War Diary	Bailleulval	23/03/1917	10/04/1917
War Diary	S.z.b.8.3	11/04/1917	13/04/1917
War Diary	Boisleux-Au-Mont	14/04/1917	15/04/1917
War Diary	Bailleulval	10/04/1917	10/04/1917
War Diary	S.Z. B.8.3	11/04/1917	13/04/1917
War Diary	Boisleux-Au-Mont	14/04/1917	19/05/1917
War Diary	Line of March	23/05/1917	31/05/1917
War Diary	G16.d.8.8	31/05/1917	31/05/1917
War Diary	Line of March	30/05/1917	31/05/1917
War Diary	G16.d.8.8	31/05/1917	15/06/1917
War Diary	G79.d.9.8	15/06/1917	29/06/1917
War Diary	Ouderdom	01/07/1917	31/07/1917
Heading	War Diary Of 30th D.A.C. For The Month Of August 1917 Vol: 21		
War Diary	Ouderdom	01/08/1917	11/08/1917
War Diary	G.9.c.5.2 Sheet 36.a	11/08/1917	15/08/1917
War Diary	Rouge Croix	15/08/1917	24/08/1917
War Diary	Dranoutre	24/08/1917	21/11/1917
War Diary	Zevecoten	27/11/1917	03/01/1918
War Diary	Godewaersvelde	04/01/1918	04/01/1918
War Diary	Morbecque	05/01/1918	05/01/1918
War Diary	Renescure	06/01/1918	10/01/1918
War Diary	Berteaucourt	12/01/1918	12/01/1918
War Diary	Hangest	13/01/1918	13/01/1918
War Diary	Roye	19/01/1918	19/01/1918
War Diary	Offoy	20/01/1918	20/02/1918
War Diary	Villers St Christophe	28/02/1918	22/03/1918
War Diary	Eppeville	22/03/1918	22/03/1918
War Diary	Esmery Hallon	23/03/1918	23/03/1918
War Diary	Ognolles	24/03/1918	24/03/1918
War Diary	Solente	24/03/1918	24/03/1918
War Diary	Champien	25/03/1918	25/03/1918
War Diary	Roiglise	25/03/1918	25/03/1918
War Diary	Beuvraignes	26/03/1918	26/03/1918
War Diary	Grivillers	26/03/1918	26/03/1918
War Diary	Faverolles	26/03/1918	26/03/1918
War Diary	Fontaine-Sous-Montdidier	27/03/1918	27/03/1918
War Diary	Mailly-Raineval	28/03/1918	28/03/1918
War Diary	Merville-au-Bois	29/03/1918	29/03/1918
War Diary	Jumel	31/03/1918	31/03/1918
War Diary	Berny-Sur-Noye	01/04/1918	04/04/1918

War Diary	Essertaux	05/04/1918	07/04/1918
War Diary	Saleux	08/04/1918	09/04/1918
War Diary	Ferm Petit Qeusnel	10/04/1918	11/04/1918
War Diary	Belloy-Sur-Somme	12/04/1918	12/04/1918
War Diary	Candas	13/04/1918	13/04/1918
War Diary	Gezaincourt	14/04/1918	14/04/1918
War Diary	P.31	16/04/1918	16/04/1918
War Diary	L.35.d.8.5	22/04/1918	22/04/1918
War Diary	L.35.D.8.5 Sheet 27	22/04/1918	25/04/1918
War Diary	L.14.b.2.5	26/04/1918	30/04/1918
War Diary	L.14.b.2.5 Sheet 27	02/05/1918	06/05/1918
War Diary	Q.13.b.4.7	08/05/1918	27/05/1918
War Diary	Racquinghem B.19.a.5.6. Sheet 36.a	15/06/1918	15/06/1918
War Diary	Sercus C.8.d.5.5	17/06/1918	25/06/1918
War Diary	Sercus	01/07/1918	02/07/1918
War Diary	P.14.b.8.6 Sheet 27	08/07/1918	27/07/1918
War Diary	P.6.c.8.8	29/07/1918	30/07/1918
War Diary	P.6.c.8.8 Sheet 27	31/07/1918	31/08/1918
War Diary	R.7.b, 3.6 Sheet 27	01/09/1918	01/09/1918
War Diary	M.2.a.2.1 Sheet 28	05/09/1918	20/09/1918
War Diary	Croix Du Poperinghe	29/09/1918	30/09/1918
War Diary	Sheet 28 Croix de Poperinghe	01/10/1918	01/10/1918
War Diary	N.28.d.9.9	02/10/1918	16/10/1918
War Diary	I.32.c.5.4	17/10/1918	18/10/1918
War Diary	Oogereet Fm	19/10/1918	19/10/1918
War Diary	Sterhoek	20/10/1918	22/10/1918
War Diary	Coyghem	24/10/1918	31/10/1918
War Diary	Sheet 29 Rolleghem	04/11/1918	06/11/1918
War Diary	Belleghem	09/11/1918	09/11/1918
War Diary	O.14.a.5.5 Sheet 29	10/11/1918	10/11/1918
War Diary	Avelghem	11/11/1918	23/11/1918
War Diary	Ruddervoorde	29/11/1918	02/12/1918
War Diary	Verlinghem	03/12/1918	03/12/1918
War Diary	Thiennes	11/12/1918	11/12/1918

WO 95
2321/8
30th Divl AMMN COLUMN
Sept 1915 - Dec 1918

30TH DIVISION
DIVL ARTILLERY

30TH DIVL AMMN COLUMN
SEPT 1915 - DEC 1918

30TH DIVISION
DIVL ARTILLERY

30th Bn

30th B.n.
Vol. I

121/7928

Dec 1915
Dec 1918

Confidential

War Diary

of

30th Divisional Ammunition Column

From 25.8.15 to 31st December 1915.

Volume I

Army Form C. 2118.

WAR DIARY
or
INTELLIGENCE SUMMARY.
(Erase heading not required.)

30th D.A.C. Dec. 1915

Place	Date	Hour	Summary of Events and Information	Remarks and references to Appendices
ST OUEN	6.12.15		Two Officers, CAPT WISEMAN & LIEUT. SMALE sent to join the 45th DAC for five days for information	
ST OUEN	11.12.15	12.0	Visit of C.R.E. to inspect progress of horse standings &c	
ST OUEN	12.12.15	12.0	Visit of C.R.A. 13th Corps.	
ST OUEN	13.12.15		ADJUTANT & R.S.M. joined 48th DAC for 4 days for information	
"	14.12.15		Hard frost - weather fine & bright	
"	15.12.15		Milder thaw.	
"	22.12.15	11.45	Visit of G.O.C. 13th CORPS - weather wet.	
"	27.12.15		Orders received for C.O. to carry out thorough reconnaissance of the town with a view to accommodating 3 Brigades R.F.A. & 1 DAC, providing horse standings & the necessary accessory buildings. To advise the work. 1 section R.E. & 1 Coy. PIONEERS arrived.	
"	28.12.15			

Army Form C. 2118.

WAR DIARY
or
INTELLIGENCE SUMMARY.
(Erase heading not required.)

30th Divisional Ammunition Column

Place	Date	Hour	Summary of Events and Information	Remarks and references to Appendices
GRANTHAM	28.8.15	12 Noon	H.Q. of Column assembled. Column organised as a Unit	JSDM
GRANTHAM	17.9.15	5.20 a.m.	Move to LARKHILL. 1st train leaves GRANTHAM 5.20 A.M. arrives AMESBURY 4 P.M. Last train arrives 5 P.M.	JSDM JSDM
LARKHILL	20.11.15	11 A.M.	Inspection of 30th Divisional Artillery by LORD DERBY	JSDM
LARKHILL	28.11.15	5.15 P.M.	Leave LARKHILL for FRANCE. 8 trains loaded AMESBURY to SOUTHAMPTON & embark on Transports. 3/4 of Column S.S. COURTFIELD, remainder on	JSDM
SOUTHAMPTON	29.11.15	4.30 P.M.	S.S. INVENTOR. Left SOUTHAMPTON 4.30 P.M. 1st part of voyage rough, arrive	MSDM
HAVRE	30.11.15	6 A.M.	at HAVRE. Disembarked, marched to Halle 3, Gare Maritime, German in Halle 3 for the night.	MSDM
HAVRE	1.12.15	5 A.M.	Entrained for DOULLENS, five trainloads, 1st train left 5 a.m. last train with headquarters 2/12/15 5 a.m. Arrive at DOULLENS detraining	MSDM
DOULLENS	2.12.15		in heavy rain, marched by road to ST OUEN, arrived 12 noon (less detachment). Weather very wet. Our mile	MSDM
ST OUEN	3.12.15			MSDM
ST OUEN	5.12.15	11.30	Conference with C.R.E. re instructions to prepare for long stay in this District. C.O. to arrange for Brick & horse standings, dining rooms, ablution rooms and horse latrines & forest-hewn & cookhouses	JSDM

T2134. Wt. W708-776. 500000. 4/15. Sir J. C. & S.

Bd. ð BJC.
= bl: 2
Tan '16

Confidential

War Diary
of
30th Divisional Ammunition Column

from 1.2.16 to 31.3.16

Volume 2.

J.P. Wheatley
Lt. Col. RFA

Original

Army Form C. 2118.

January 1916

WAR DIARY

or

~~INTELLIGENCE SUMMARY.~~

(Erase heading not required.)

30 Divisional Ammunition Column

Instructions regarding War Diaries and Intelligence Summaries are contained in F. S. Regs., Part II. and the Staff Manual respectively. Title pages will be prepared in manuscript.

Place	Date	Hour	Summary of Events and Information	Remarks and references to Appendices
ST OUEN	1.1.16	1.20 AM	Message received. FRENCH near ARRAS report suspicious movements of GERMANS. Proceed & second message. STAND TO. on ALARM POSTS	appx
"	"	10 AM	Further message. Carry on as usual.	appx
"	3.1.16		Instructions received to prepare scheme for billeting 3 Brigades R.F.A. & 1 D.A.C. in ST OUEN	appx
"	5.1.16	12 noon	Inspection of horse standings by C.R.A. 13th CORPS	appx
"	5.1.16		March tables for impending move received	appx
"	7.1.16	5.30 pm	Lecture on LOOS by Lt Col TUDOR at VIGNACOURT.	appx
"	10.1.16	9 a.m.	No 1 Section under CAPT WISEMAN started for CHIPILLY	appx
"	"	2.30 pm	Billeting scheme completed & handed to C.R.A. 30 Div. ARTY	appx
"	19.1.16	9 AM	Commenced march to CHIPILLY. O.C. 30 DAC in command of Column No 13, consisting of Sections + MOBILE VET SECTION 24.3. 30 DAC with Brigade Ammunition Columns 148, 149, 150 & 151 Brigades RFA & Head of Column arrived TALMAS 12 noon. Route via BERTEAUCOURT, HALLOY, WARGNIES, NAOURS, TOLL	appx
TALMAS			B.A.C's billeted at TALMAS. DAC at NAOURS. M.V.S. at WARGNIES. Weather fine but rain during night	appx
NAOURS	20.1.16	8.30	March continued. Started 8.30 A.M. Route via SEPTENVILLE, PIERREGOT, MOLLIENS AUX	appx
NAOURS			BOIS, ST GRATIEN, PONT NOYELLES. BAC's & M.V.S. billeted at PONT NOYELLES. Head of Column	appx
PONT NOYELLES	20.1.16	11.30	arrived 11.30 A.M. D.A.C. billeted at LA HOUSSOYE. arrived 2 A.M.	appx
LA HOUSSOYE	"	2 PM		appx

Original

Army Form C. 2118.

WAR DIARY

~~INTELLIGENCE~~ SUMMARY.

(Erase heading not required.)

January 1916

30th Divisional Ammunition Column

Instructions regarding War Diaries and Intelligence Summaries are contained in F.S. Regs., Part II. and the Staff Manual respectively. Title pages will be prepared in manuscript.

Place	Date	Hour	Summary of Events and Information	Remarks and references to Appendices
PONT NOYELLES	20.1.16	12 noon	Driver RENSHAW, 149th BAC RFA accidentally drowned whilst watering horses	
CHIPILLY	21.1.16	12 noon	March conducted. Started 8.30 a.m. Route via CORBIE, VAUX, SAILLY, LAURETTE, SAILLY LAURETTE, CHIPILLY. First unit arrived here 12 noon. BAC's proceeded to permanent positions. DAC to Billets. Lost over 20 shoes vacated by 5th Division & commenced to prepare their Quarters during rather marsh from Roads Lines. Deep mud at CHIPILLY.	
"	24.1.16		Capt. F. WISEMAN (O.C. No 1 Section) admitted to Hospital. 2/Lieut S. MOLYNEUX taken over command temporarily.	
"	27.1.16	12 noon	Visit of Inspection by GEN. FRY.	
"	28.1.16	9 p.m.	Heavy gunfire heard from E. & S.E. Orders received that all men are to sleep in boots & puttees with rifles & equipment beside them.	
"	29.1.16		Heavy gunfire continued all day. Three rounds live ammunition to be issued out along to each Brigade Ammunition Column in the Division.	

30th D.3
A. C.
Vol. 3

Confidential

War Diary

of

30th Divisional Ammunition Column

J P Wheatley Lt Col RFA

from 1. Feb. 1916   to 25 Feb. 1916

(Volume III)

WAR DIARY or INTELLIGENCE SUMMARY

Army Form C. 2118.

30 DIVISIONAL AMMUNITION COLUMN

February 1916

Place	Date	Hour	Summary of Events and Information	Remarks and references to Appendices
CHIPILLY	1.2.16		Weather bright & frosty	
	30.1.16	11.30	Orders received from C.R.A. to supply ammunition to 37th & 65th How: Batteries & 119th 120th & 121st 18pr Batteries.	
"	6.2.16		Heavy indents for ammunition have been received daily from all Brigades during the past week	
"	8.2.16		3 Waggons with teams & drivers, 1 Corpl: 1 Bomb: & 1 A/Bomb: detached to accompany C.Batty. 151st Brigade, & 1 section B.A.C. to form 51st Brigade.	
"	10.2.16		Baths opened for men of the Column	
"	14.2.16		Weather very wet & stormy	
"	18.2.16		1 Officer & 14 men sent to French Gunnery School VAUNEUREUX	
"	20.2.16		Instructions received for Column to move to SAILLY-LE-SEC on Monday 28.2.16	
"	25.2.16		Heavy snowfall all day.	
"	26.2.16		Thaw.	
"	28.2.16	2 am	Move to SAILLY-LE-SEC cancelled by telephone message from 31st DIV.ARTY	

Original

February 1916

2.

WAR DIARY
or
INTELLIGENCE SUMMARY.
(Erase heading not required.)

Army Form C. 2118.

Note of amount of ammunition issued from Depots since arriving in France.

Place	Date	Hour	18 Pr.		4.5" How.		S.A.A	Remarks and references to Appendices
			Shrapnel	H.E.	Shrapnel	H.E.		
			December 1915					
ST OUEN	Round		576	—	—	1608	233,000	
			January 1916					
Destroying	9.1.16		—	—	—	690	86,000	
"	16.1.16		—	—	—	258	—	
"	23.1.16		1376	248	—	208	1000	
"	30.1.16		2208	1404	—	1646	458,000	
			3784	1652		2742	544,000	

J.M.Minchin Lt.Col R.A.
Com 30

Original

3

WAR DIARY
or
INTELLIGENCE SUMMARY.
(Erase heading not required.)

February 1916   Army Form C. 2118.

Instructions regarding War Diaries and Intelligence Summaries are contained in F. S. Regs., Part II. and the Staff Manual respectively. Title pages will be prepared in manuscript.

Place	Date	Hour	Summary of Events and Information	Remarks and references to Appendices
			Ammunition issued for Feb 1916	
			18 pr. 4.5" How.	
			SHRAPNEL H.E. SHRAPNEL H.E. S.A.A.	
CHIPILLY				
Week ending	6.2.16		6536 248 — 3058 226.000	
"	13.2.16		2148 604 — 1604 407.000	
"	20.2.16		2178 228 — 548 298.000	
"	27.2.16		568 168 — 718 3000	
			11430 1248 — 5928 934000	

M.J. Wheatley Lt.
Comdg 38 B.D.S.C.

30 Dws
A. Col
Vol 4

War Diary
of
30th Divisional Ammunition Column.

Volume IV

from 1st March 1916 to 31st March 1916

J.W. Wheatley
Lt. Col. R.F.A.

30th D.A.C. March 1916 Army Form C. 2118.

WAR DIARY or INTELLIGENCE SUMMARY

Place	Date	Hour	Summary of Events and Information	Remarks and references to Appendices
CHIPILLY	29.2.16		Ammunition supply in future to be from a Large Stationed at ETINEHEM consisting complement of a SUB PARK. Being to remain stationary & to be replenished as required by another Large from CORBIE. 1 Officer & 15 men detached for duty of receiving & issuing ammunition in Large	
"	5.3.16		2/Lieuts. W.G. FREND & A.G. BISHOP arrived from ENGLAND, posted to this Column	NOM
"	9.3.16		2/Lieut C.T. BARTON arrived. 1 Corp: 1 Bomb: & 8 men sent to French Mortar School	NOM
"	12.3.16		R.S.M. C.F. TURNER commissioned 2/Lieut & posted to this Column	NOM
"	19.3.16		2/Lieut. J.C. Watson struck off the strength	MB9
	20.3.16		Lt. C. Catell. Posted from 149 Artz & took over command of this Section.	MB9
	23.3.16		Column moved from Chipilly to Bussy les Daours.	MB9
BUSSY	28.3.16		2/Lt E.W. Pemberton joined from Base.	MB9
	27.3.16		Column moved from Bussy les Daours to Argoeuvres.	MB9
ARGOEUVRES				

30th D.A.C.

March 1916

Original

Army Form C. 2118.

WAR DIARY
or
INTELLIGENCE SUMMARY.
(Erase heading not required.)

Place	Date	Hour	Summary of Events and Information	Remarks and references to Appendices
			Ammunition issued March 1916	
			A Ax B Bx SAA	
	Week ending 5-3-16		1673 192 — 650 35000	
	" 12.3.16		668 293 — 332 718000	
	" 19.3.16		1908 151 56 760 43000	
	" 26.3.16		nil nil nil 46 nil	

W.J. Wheatley Major
Lt. Col.
Comdg 30 D.A.C.

30 D A C
Vol. 5

War Diary
of
30th Divisional Ammunition Column

Volume 5

from
1st April 1916
to
30th April 1916

J.W. Weekley
Lt Col RFA

30.D.A.C.

April 1916

WAR DIARY
or
INTELLIGENCE SUMMARY.
(Erase heading not required.)

Army Form C. 2118.

Place	Date	Hour	Summary of Events and Information	Remarks and references to Appendices
ARGOEUVRES	3.4.16		2nd Lieut W.G. FREND R.F.A. posted & transferred to 150th B.A. R.F.A.	Appx I
"	6.4.16		Portion of Column inspected by G.O.C. 30th Division with remainder of Divl Arty not in the line.	Appx II
"	7.4.16		No.1 Section returned to CHIPILLY for service in the line, with all wagons for supply of 4.5" How: Ammunition	Appx III
"	8.4.16		Inspection of lines, harness etc by G.O.C. 13th Corps	Appx IV
"	17.4.16		2nd Lieut C.T. BARTON posted to French Horse Bath: returned off work Effect from 9.3.16	Appx V
"	17.4.16		15 Wagons of No 2 Section under 2/Lieut SMALE sent to SAILLY LAURETTE to assist with work on roads	Appx VI
"	19.4.16		No 100349 Gr JAMES McDONALD killed on LONGPRÉ - ARGOEUVRES Road by a kick from a horse	Appx VII
"	20.4.16		Funeral of Gr JAMES McDONALD at ARGOEUVRES	Appx VIII
"	21.4.16		2/Lieut A. KAY with 3 Gr sent to Trad Hors School VAUX	Appx IX
CHIPILLY	24.4.16		No1 Section moved from CHIPILLY to LA NEUVILLE BRAY	Appx X
ARGOEUVRES	28.4.16		Inspection of horses, harness, wagons & billets by C.R.A.	Appx XI

R.W. Murdoch Lt Col
Comdg 30th D.A.C.

30th Div'nl. Arty.
No. ----------------
    1462.

The attached letters and tables regarding the re-organization of the Div.Amn.Col: and the abolition of Bde.Amn.Columns are forwarded for information.

The 148th Bde.Amn.Col: less Officers, will become No. 4 Section, ('B' Echelon), Div.Amn.Col: and will be made up to Establishment by repostings from the Amn.Columns of the other Brigades as shown on the attached statement. This unit will be handed over to Div.Amn.Col: intact as it now stands and no exchanges of horses and personnel will be made. If the 148th Brigade wishes to make any exchanges it will do so from the Bde.Amn.Columns of 149, 150 & 151. Captain H. Wilkins will command it and three subalterns will be posted under orders from R.A., HdQrs.

The three existing Sections of the Div.Amn.Col: will become the 'A' Echelon and will similarly be made up to their new Establishment by repostings from the Bde.Amn.Columns as shown in the statement.

'A' Echelon will be quartered in the BOIS DE TAILLES and 1, 2 and 3 Sections will take over the lines allotted to 149, 150 and 151 Bde.Amn.Columns respectively. 'B' Echelon will be quartered in CHIPILLY in the lines now occupied by No.2 Section, Div.Amn.Col:, which moves to the BOIS DE TAILLES.

Repostings and transfers in men, horses, and vehicles will be made forthwith to have effect from the 16th instant. Brigades will by that date also complete their batteries to establishment and make such exchanges in men and horses as they think desirable. The numbers (personnel only) to be posted will not exceed those shown as deficient on A.F. B.213 plus 5% to cover anticipated wastage. In addition Brigades will also post to

-2-.

batteries from Bde.Amn.Col: sufficient N.C.O's and men to replace those earmarked for 2 Heavy Trench Mortar Batteries, (see letter on this subject No.1501 dated 14-5-16).

When these repostings have been effected, the following numerical returns will be rendered to this office without fail by 9 am. 17th inst:-

1. Surplus Personnel for despatch to ABBEVILLE.
2. "   Horses, showing whether R. or D.
3. "   Vehicles, giving description.
4. Required to complete, in detail, (Div.Amn.Col: only). } 6 pm 16-5-16.

If any vehicles cannot be horsed to ABBEVILLE they will be handed in to D.A.D.O.S. in sufficient time to admit of their being evacuated by the 18th inst.

At noon 16th inst. the responsibility for supply of Ammunition will devolve on the Div.Amn.Col: as follows:-

Artillery Ammunition.

No.1 Section - Centre Group - 18 pr. & 4.5" Ammn.
No.2.Section - Right   "   -   do.
No.3. "   - In reserve.

Infantry.

No.1 Section - 21st Infantry Brigade -)
No.2. "   - 89th   do.   -) S.A.A. &c.
No.3   "   - 90th   do.   -)

The 82nd Bde.Amn.Col: becomes No.1 Section 18th Div. Amn.Col: and will continue to be responsible for supply of 18 pr. and 4.5" Ammunition to the Left Group.

The Ammunition at present in possession of 149 & 150 Bde.Amn.Columns will be handed over to No.1 and No.2 Sections Div.Amn.Col: respectively and that in possession of 151 (How.) Bde.Amn.Col: will be equally divided (as far as possible) between No.1, 2 & 3 Sections Div.Amn.Col: As the Sections will be responsible for ammunition supply from 12 noon on 16th instant, the ammunition with Bde.Amn.Columns should be handed over, as above, before that date.

All horses will be handed over to Sections of Div.Amn.

-3-.

Col: as complete turns out, i.e. with harness and appointments.

The personnel etc of 149th Bde.Amn.Col: and half that of 150th Bde.Amn.Col: remaining after all repostings and exchanges have been made, will proceed by march route to ABBEVILLE on the 18th instant as directed and that of 151st Bde.Amn.Col and the remainder of 150th Bde.Amn.Col:, on the 23rd idem.

Indents for rations and forage for the three days referred to, will therefore be submitted, on the 16th May, (<u>or sooner if possible</u>) and 20th May respectively by the units concerned.

Instructions will be issued later, in a separate letter, with regard to the various wagon fatigues at present carried out by the Div.Amn.Col:

The Headquarters of the Div.Amn.Col: will move to CHIPILLY and be quartered there with No.4 Section under arrangements to be made forthwith by the O.C., Div.Amn.Col: in conjunction with the Town Major there.

C.G.F. Webb

Captain, R.A.,

14-5-1916.   Staff Captain, 30th Divisional Artillery.

SECRET.

O.B./818

General Staff, Fourth Army
163 (G).

First Army,
Second Army,
Third Army,
Fourth Army.

   In continuation of G.H.Q. letter No. O.B.818 of the 28th April, the following further measures of re-organisation in connection with the Divisional Artillery will be undertaken :-

 (a) <u>Formation of Mixed Brigades</u> -

  (i) In the 8 old Regular Divisions and in the Lahore Divisional Artillery (attached to 3rd Canadian Division), the howitzer brigades will be broken up, one battery of four howitzers being added to each of the 18-pounder brigades.

   The artillery of these Divisions will then consist of three mixed Brigades constituted as follows:-

   Two Brigades of three 6-gun 18-pounder batteries and one battery of four 4.5-inch howitzers.
   One brigade of two 6-gun 18-pounder batteries and one battery of four 4.5-inch howitzers.

   The Headquarters of the Howitzer Brigades will be withdrawn.

  (ii). In all other Divisions one howitzer battery will be substituted for one 18-pounder battery in each of the 18-pounder brigades.

   The three 18-pounder batteries thus displaced will form the fourth brigade under the former howitzer brigade headquarters.

   The artillery of Divisions with 12 howitzers will then consist of three mixed brigades and one 18-pounder brigade constituted as follows:-

Three mixed brigades ...	Three 18-pdr batteries and one howitzer battery.
One 18-pounder brigade ...	Three 18-pounder batteries.

   The artillery of the Divisions with 16 howitzers will consist of four mixed brigades each brigade containing three 18-pounder batteries and one howitzer battery.

 Changes in the nomenclature of batteries necessitated by transfers from one brigade to another will be reported to General Headquarters shewing in each case the old and

the/

2.

the new designation. The letter "D" will be assigned to the howitzer battery in each brigade.

The above measures will be undertaken as and when the military situation permits, under arrangements to be made by Army Commanders.

    (b) Re-organization of the system of ammunition supply within the Division -

In order to meet the changed conditions consequent on the growth of the Army, and to provide an organisation which will be more manageable and more economical than that at present existing, the Commander-in-Chief has decided -

(a) To abolish the Brigade Ammunition Columns as such;
(b) To re-constitute the Divisional Ammunition Columns into Divisional Columns, of two echelons each, composed as follows:-

Headquarters,
"A" echelon, consisting of 3 sections
    (Nos: 1, 2, and 3 Sections)
"B" echelon, consisting of 1 section
    (No. 4 Section.)

The Headquarters and "A" echelon are designed to accompany the Division closely at all times. "B" echelon will follow the Division if circumstances permit, but is detachable under Corps control when necessary.

2.   Tables showing the new War Establishment of a Divisional Ammunition Column are attached.

3.   This re-organization will be commenced forthwith, the surplus personnel, horses and vehicles, being desposed of under orders to be issued by the Adjutant General and Quartermaster General.

                                  Sd. R. BUTLER, M.G.

General Headquarters,   for Lieutenant General
    6th May, 1916.   C. G. S.

DIVISIONAL AMMUNITION COLUMN.

War Establishment.

	Personnel.							Horses.						
	Officers.	Warrant Officers Clerks.	S/Sgts & Sgts. Artificers.	Trumpeters.	Rank & file.		TOTAL.	Riding.	Draught.	Pack.	Heavy Draught.	TOTAL.	Bicycles.	Motor Cycles.
Headquarters, (excluding attached)	2	1	-	2	-	-	24	29	7	28	-	-	35	-	-
Attached.	1	-	-	4	-	-	3	8	5	-	-	-	5	-	-
Nos. 1, 2 & 3 Sections.	9	3	-	15	27	-	459	513	57	582	-	-	639	-	-
No. 4 Section.	4	1	-	7	12	-	236	260	21	310	-	-	331	-	-
Total Column (excluding attached)	15	5	-	24	39	-	719	802	85	920	-	-	1005	-	-
Total Column (including attached)	16	5	-	28	39	-	722	810	90	920	-	-	1010	-	-
Each Section	3	1		5	9		153	171	19	194			213	1	-

DIVISIONAL AMMUNITION COLUMN.

War Establishment. (continued).

DETAIL	Personnel								Horses					Bicycles	Motor Bicycles
	Officers	Warrant Officers	Clerks	S/Sgts & Sgts	Artificers	Trumpeters	Rank & File	TOTAL	Riding	Draught	Hy.Draught	Pack	TOTAL		
COMPOSITION IN DETAIL															
Headquarters -															
Lieutenant Colonel.	1							1	2				2		
Adjutant	1							1	2				2		
Sergeant Major		1						1	1				1		
Artillery Clerk			1					1							
Artillery Clerk			1					1							
Battery Qr.Mr.Sgt.				1				1	1				1		
Clerk							1	1							
Gunners							1	1	1				1		
Orderlies for M.O.(c)							3	3		4			4		
(for vehicles							10	10		20			20		
Drivers(For spare draught horses							2	2		4			4		
(spare							2	2							
Batmen (d)							5	5							
Total Headquarters (excluding attached)	2	1	2				24	29	7	28			35		
Attached -															
R.A.M.C.(includes personnel for water duties).	1						(e)3	4	1				1		
Sergeants,A.V.C.(f)				4				4	4				4		
Drivers, A.S.C. (train transport).							13	13			26		26		
Total Headquarters (including attached)	3	1	6				27	37	12	28			40		

(b). Attached to A.G's Office at the Base.
(c). 3 men (1 an acting bombardier) trained to the duties are placed under the orders of the medical officer. The gunners drive the carts for medical equipment.
(d). All batmen are fully armed and trained soldiers, and are available for duty in the ranks.
(e). Includes a corporal
(f). One per section.

DIVISIONAL AMMUNITION COLUMN.

War Establishment. (Continued.)

(ii) Transport. (Continued.)

(j) Riders will be detailed as required from rank and file.
(k) Medical Officer's Orderlies.
(l) Arrangements may, if necessary, be made for the carriage of the Headquarter's baggage in the baggage wagons or wagons of one or more sections.
(m) Provided from the Divisional Train.

NOTE :-

In Divisions having 16 Howitzers, the following will be added:-

"A" Echelon .. Wagons, Ammunition with limbers... 4.
                Drivers.........................12.
                Horses..........................24.

"B" Echelon.... G.S. Wagons..................... 4.
                Drivers.........................12.
                Horses..........................24.

Under the present system, the following personnel and vehicles are EMPLOYED in a Division for Ammunition supply. Figures approximate only.

DETAIL	Personnel							Horses					Bicycles	Motor Cycles
	Officers	Warrant Offrs. Clerks	Staff Sergts. & Sergeants.	Artificers	Trumpeters	Rank & File	TOTAL	Riding	Draught.	Hy. Draught	Pack	TOTAL		
OLD SYSTEM –														
3 F.A.Bde.Ammn.Columns	12	3		15	24	402	456	60	516			576		
How.Bde. Ammn. Column (3 batteries)	2	1		3	7	77	90	15	88			103		
Divnl. Ammn. Column	11	4		8	30	468	521	46	590			636		
Attached	1			3		4	8	5				5		
	26	8		29	61	951	1075	126	1194			1320		
NEW SYSTEM –	16	5		28	39	722	810	90	920			1010		
Nett saving	10	3		1	22	229	265	36	274			310		

VEHICLES.

	Ammn. Wagons.	L.G.S.	G.S.	Maltese	Water	Bicycles
Old system	60	15	131	1	6	9
New system	60	15	87	2	3	14
Nett reduction			44		3	
Increase				1		5

30th Divnl. Arty.
No. ———————————
            1462.

G.H.Q. No. O.B./818.
Fourth Army No. 163 (G)
XIII Corps No. Q.C.1106.
30th Divn. O.4888.

Secret

Fourth Army.
——————————

With reference to G.H.Q. letter No. O.B./818 of the 6th instant.; a misunderstanding appears to have arisen in certain quarters regarding the organisation of the new Divisional Ammunitions Columns.

The reasons for the change may be summarized as follows:-

As a result of the growth of the Army in the Field, the Corps has replaced the Division as the unit for marching and fighting. The restricted fronts that will be available for allotment to Corps in any probable forward move, the small number of roads, and the greater density of the troops with their consequent disposal in depth, combine to render the retention of two ammunition echelons under Divisional control no longer practicable.

The new Divisional Ammunition Columns which are now being formed have been organised in two echelons; the 'A' echelons being designed to accompany their Divisions closely at all times; and 'B' echelons being available either to accompany their own Divisions, if the circumstances and available road space render such a course desirable, or to be detached under Corps control.

The 'A' echelons are divided into three sections for purposes of administration only, and these sections are not intended to serve any particular Infantry or Artillery brigade. The Column as a whole serves the Division as a whole. With the reduced amount of ammunition carried it is essential that this Column be treated as a pool; the affiliation of sections to particular brigades, or the local re-formation of sections on a different basis is contrary to the principles underlying the organisation and is not to be permitted. The establishment as laid down will be strictly followed.

General Headquarters.
22nd May 1916.

(Sd.) J.Burnett Stuart, B.G., for
           Lieutenant General, C.G.S.

2.

———————————————

For information.

As a matter of convenience only No's.1 and 2 Sections, 30th Div.Amn.Col: are now supplying the ammunition to the Right and Centre Groups.

All 3 sections of 'A' echelon will, however, always be prepared to supply ammunition to any battery in the Division ff called upon to do so.

C.S.F.Webb

Captain, R.A.,

26-5-16.   Staff Captain, 30th Divisional Artillery.

30 D.A.C.
Vol 6

War Diary
of
30 Divisional Ammunition Column

Volume VI

from
1st May 1916
to
31 May 1916

JDW Heneky
Lt Col RFA
Comd 30 DAC

Army Form C. 2118.

WAR DIARY
INTELLIGENCE SUMMARY
(Erase heading not required.)

3059. D.A.C.   May 1916

Original

Place	Date	Hour	Summary of Events and Information	Remarks and references to Appendices
ARGOEUVRES	1/5/16	11 AM	Inspection of horses & billets by ERA 30th Divn	App IV
"	5/5/16	5.30	Move to SAILLY LAURETTE via LONGPRÉ - AMIENS - DAOURS - AUDIGNY - CORBIE	App IV
SAILLY LAURETTE	11.5.16	9 AM	Move to CHIPILLY	App IV
		12 nn	Reorganisation of DAC. Abolition of BAC's & formation of A & B Echelons. DAC then reconstructed involves the increase of the personnel of the Column from 529 to 810, horses from 641 to 1010, & vehicles from 100 to 168. In future the three echelons in return of the DAC forming A Echelon will carry out the duties formerly carried out by the BAC's of the 145, 148, 150 & 151 Brigades. B Echelon & the original DAC forming Nos 1 & 2 Echelons of the reorganised DMC for the present of Nos 1 & 2 Echelons will supply the Right & Centre group & No 3 Echelon in reserve. Nos 2 & 3 Echelons move from CHIPILLY to BOIS DE TAILLÉ. A & (B Echelon) formed at CHIPILLY with Capt WILKINS REA. Evacuation of waggons & surplus mules & equipment when No 1 Section moves from LA NEUVILLE to 4.15 & 2.15 men BRAY	App IV App IV App IV App IV App IV
	13/5/16 12.5.16			App IV App IV

Original

30 J.A.C.

Army Form C. 2118.

WAR DIARY
or
INTELLIGENCE SUMMARY.
(Erase heading not required.)

Instructions regarding War Diaries and Intelligence Summaries are contained in F. S. Regs., Part II. and the Staff Manual respectively. Title pages will be prepared in manuscript.

Place	Date	Hour	Summary of Events and Information	Remarks and references to Appendices
BRAY	18.5.16		One driver wounded – Shrapnel.	J.M.W.
CHIPILLY	20.5.16	10 A.M.	Headquarters & B. Echelon move to SAILLY LAURETTE	J.M.W.
	23.5.16		2/Lieut SMALE admitted to Hospital	J.M.W.
SUZANNE	20.5.16		One driver wounded. Shrapnel.	J.M.W.
SAILLY LAURETTE	22.5.16		No.1 Section moves from BRAY to BOIS DE TAILLES	J.M.W.
"	25.5.16		2/Lieut DOAK admitted to Hospital; sent to Rest Camp.	J.M.W.

J.D. Wheatley
Lt. Col. R.J.A.C.
Com'g 30 J.A.C.

Army Form C. 2118.

30 D A C

WAR DIARY
or
INTELLIGENCE SUMMARY.
(Erase heading not required.)

Instructions regarding War Diaries and Intelligence Summaries are contained in F. S. Regs., Part II. and the Staff Manual respectively. Title pages will be prepared in manuscript.

Original

Ammunition issued by 30 D A C May 1916.

Place	Date	Hour	Summary of Events and Information						Remarks and references to Appendices
				A	Ax.	E	Bx	SAA	
Week ending									
	MAY 14			17872	5292	—	6274	86000	
"	21			1332	388	—	814	274000	
"	28			160	240	—	1056	89000	
				19364	5920	—	8144	454000	

M J Macintosh Lt Col RFA
Lt Col. 30 D.A.C.
Comg

Officer i/c
    A.O's office Base.

I regret that this War Diary
for June was not forwarded
earlier owing to its having been
mislaid. Future diaries will
be sent through Division as
ordered

J.D Wheatley
                    Lt Col RA
        Comg 30 D.A.C.

23.7.16

WAR DIARY
or
INTELLIGENCE SUMMARY

War Diary

of

35th Divisional Ammunition Column

VOLUME VII

J.M.M. Mackay
Lt Col RFA

from
June 1916

30 June 1916

30 Div Am Col
Vol 7

June

30. DAC

WAR DIARY or INTELLIGENCE SUMMARY

Army Form C. 2118.

June 1916

Place	Date	Hour	Summary of Events and Information	Remarks and references to Appendices
SAILLY LAURETTE	1.6.16	5.30 p.m.	Visit of G.O.C. 30 Division	appx
BOIS DES TAILLES	3.6.16		Head Quarters DAC move to BOIS DES TAILLES near ETINEHEM (K.24.d.9.2)	appx
"	31.5.16		CAPT. F. NOAKES + 2nd LIEUT E.B. WEINEL attached to DAC	appx
"	6.6.16		2nd LIEUT H.H.M. DAWSON posted from DAC to 148 Bde RFA	appx
"	10.6.16		2/LIEUT E.S. SMALE invalided to England struck off the strength of the Column	appx
"	14.6.16		2/LIEUT S. MOLYNEUX posted from DAC to A/157 Bde RFA 2/LIEUT S.S. EVANS to DAC	appx
"	20.6.16		No. 9533 B.Q.M.S. F. FROST C/149 Bde confirmed in appointment as Acting R.S.M. (1st Class W.O.) with effect from date of taking up his duties & posted to DAC	appx
"	"		2/LIEUT A.K. posted from 30 DAC to V/30. Trench Mortar Batt from 20/6/15	appx
"	"		2/LIEUT F.H. BISHOP. RFA posted to 30 DAC with effect from 20/6/16	appx
"	23.6.16	11 A.M.	A. Echelon moved with Headquarters from BOIS DES TAILLES to SAILLY LAURETTE	appx
"	"		B. Echelon from SAILLY LAURETTE to SAILLY LE SEC	appx
SAILLY LAURETTE	"		2/Lieut S.S. EVANS posted to 1st Brigade RFA pending 2/Lieut S. MOLYNEUX to 148 Bde cancelled.	appx

Original

30. D.A.C.

June 1916.

Army Form C. 2118.

WAR DIARY
or
INTELLIGENCE SUMMARY.
(Erase heading not required.)

Place	Date	Hour	Summary of Events and Information	Remarks and references to Appendices
			Ammunition issued through 30 D.A.C. June 1916.	
			A. A× B× 2cy Shells 4.5"	
Week ending				
4. 6. 16			— — — —	
11. 6. 16			9317. 3304. 2744. —	
18. 6. 16			36756. 11501. 10304. 1100.	
25. 6. 16			29580. 9036. 5268. —	
			75653. 23,841. 18,316. 1100.	

30 July
D.A.R.
Vol 8

WAR DIARY
or
INTELLIGENCE SUMMARY

War Diary

of

30 Divisional Ammunition Column

Volume VIII

from   to
1.7.16   31.7.16

J S Wolseley
Lt Col RFA

Army Form C. 2118.

30th D.A.C. WAR DIARY or INTELLIGENCE SUMMARY. original

(Erase heading not required.)

Instructions regarding War Diaries and Intelligence Summaries are contained in F.S. Regs., Part II. and the Staff Manual respectively. Title pages will be prepared in manuscript.

Place	Date	Hour	Summary of Events and Information	Remarks and references to Appendices
SAILLY LAURETTE	10-7-16		Move to BOIS DES TAILLES ETINEHEM. B Echelon to SAILLY LAURETTE	MOW
	11/7/16		M/O OLDHAM killed in action	MOW
	12.7.16		Forward dump established at CEYLON WOOD in charge of 2/Lieut. M.SHEFFORD	MOW
K.6.c. F.26.a	16.7.16		A & B Echelon move to new dumps on BRAY – ALBERT Road	MOW
	19.7.16		Exchanged LOCKFRIDT NORDENFELDT 5.7 Cm gun brought in by party in charge of 2/Lieut EMBERSON	MOW
	20.7.16		Captured '77 mm gun brought in by party under 2/Lieut. ORMEROD. B.B. Column relieved by 35th D.A.C. C.24.3 Sections reorganising under orders of O.C. 35 D.A.C. Nos 1 & 4 Sections moved to BOIS DES TAILLES	MOW MOW MOW
K.18.d.	21.7.16			
"	13-7-16		One Driver wounded by shrapnel in action	MOW
"	19.7.16		One Driver wounded by shrapnel in action	MOW
"	22-7-16		One Driver killed by a fall from a horse	MOW
"	24-7-16		Captured '77 m.m. gun & 1 Q.F. Amm. wagon brought in by party under 2/Lieut 13/13 ORMEROD	MOW
	25-7-16		Captured '77 gun brought in by party under Lieut EMBERSON	MOW

J.M.M.Keagley

30 DAC

Army Form C. 2118.

engagement

WAR DIARY
or
INTELLIGENCE SUMMARY
(Erase heading not required.)

Place	Date	Hour	Summary of Events and Information	Remarks and references to Appendices

On the night of July 21.22. a party of 20 men under Lieut A.W. EMBERSON & L3780 Bdr. J.C. THOMPSON volunteered to go to MONTAUBAN de Picardy in captured German lines. While a gun was being removed from its emplacement a heavy fire was opened on the party & the men were scattered. They were rallied by L⁺ EMBERSON & Bdr. THOMPSON who conducted them to a place of safety. The chains removed exposed to fire & a H.E. shell burst close to them. The convenion throwing them off their meets which extend - L⁺ EMBERSON advised of this type others. The gun collected & the crown & found a shelter for them - In returning to the main party he was blown into a crater by the explosion of a shell & half buried. Though suffering severely from the effects of gas & belonging shell he stimulated & encouraged his party & they carried on the gun & throughout in the face of the damnable. They remained in the spot throughout the following day.

J.M. Meardley
L⁺ Col. R.F.A

Army Form C. 2118.

Original

WAR DIARY
or
INTELLIGENCE SUMMARY.
(Erase heading not required.)

Instructions regarding War Diaries and Intelligence Summaries are contained in F. S. Regs., Part II. and the Staff Manual respectively. Title pages will be prepared in manuscript.

Place	Date	Hour	Summary of Events and Information	Remarks and references to Appendices
			During the period from 11.6.16 to 23.7.16 — in preparation for & in course of the attack on Montauban & the surrounding country the following ammunition was handled by the 30 D.A.C.	
			A. 161,349 rounds. Ax 61,213. Bx 44,516. Lackt. 1100. Tunni. 100 The weight calculated at 18pr. 20 boxes to the ton. 4.5" 24 to the ton = 18pr. 3032 tons. 4.5 959 tons. a total of 3991 tons. In addition to this a very large quantity of trench mortar bombs, grenades & R.S.A. have been handled, amounting roughly to approximately the same weight— No. of rounds per gun in the Division 18pr. 5053 4.5" 3834	

Gpt M Healy Lt Col
p/o RFA
Comm'g 30 July

Army Form C. 2118.

Original

30 D.A.C.

WAR DIARY
or
INTELLIGENCE SUMMARY.
(Erase heading not required.)

Place	Date	Hour	Summary of Events and Information	Remarks and references to Appendices
			Ammunition issued through 30th D.A.C. July 1916	
			4.5" Previous	
2. 7. 16			16908 5211 2510 —	
9. 7. 16			17660 4577 5995 100	
16. 7. 16			31028 17000 12238 —	
23. 7. 16			40100 10584 3454 —	
30. 7. 16			nil nil nil —	
			105696 37372 26500 100	

30th Divisional Artillery.

30th DIVISIONAL AMMUNITION COLUMN R.F.A.

AUGUST 1916T

30 D.A.C.

August 1916

Army Form C. 2118.

WAR DIARY
or
INTELLIGENCE SUMMARY
(Erase heading not required.)

Instructions regarding War Diaries and Intelligence Summaries are contained in F.S. Regs., Part II. and the Staff Manual respectively. Title pages will be prepared in manuscript.

Place	Date	Hour	Summary of Events and Information	Remarks and references to Appendices
BOIS DES TAILLES	3.8.16	8 a.m	Move to DAOURS via CORBIE - LA NEUVILLE, arrived 12.30	
DAOURS	5.8.16		Column move to LONGUEAU & SALEUX to entrain with remainder of Divisional Artillery	
TANNAY	6.8.16		Column arrive at MERVILLE, THIENNES & BERGUETTE detrain & proceed by road to concentrate at TANNAY	
TANNAY	7.8.16	3 pm	Conference of CO's, Adjutants & BC's at H.Q.R.A. ST VENANT	
TANNAY	8.8.16	10.15	Visit of G.O.C. 30 Div to Column to address the men	
	9.8.16	9.30	Inspection of horses by D.D.R. & D.D.V.S.	
	11.8.16	12.0	Column moves to BETHUNE - taken over ammn supply from 39 Dl A.C. Right group only to be supplied	
BETHUNE	14.8.16		No 3 Section placed under orders of O.C. 3rd D.A.C. for supply of ammn to Battns of 30th D.A. forming Left group of 1st D.A. A party of men from H.Q. D.A.C. has been employed in forming an unexploded shell fired at Bethune on 5.8.16. 4 feet in garden behind No 15 RUE de L'UNIVERSITÉ pierced under the wall & has been buried in a circus & found just below the wall 6 meters from where it first proved inside. The diameter of the shell is 38 cm. Length 138 cm. 3 driving bands at base. 1.89 cwts from base. Base fuse No 1133. The shell is 3 meters below surface of ground.	

Original
30 D A C
Aug 1916

Army Form C. 2118.

WAR DIARY
or
INTELLIGENCE SUMMARY.
(Erase heading not required.)

Instructions regarding War Diaries and Intelligence Summaries are contained in F. S. Regs., Part II. and the Staff Manual respectively. Title pages will be prepared in manuscript.

Place	Date	Hour	Summary of Events and Information	Remarks and references to Appendices
BETHUNE.	20.8.16	4 pm	Visit of inspection by G.O.C. R.A. XI Corps. — Nos. 3. & 4 Lectures inspected	

J.B. Westby ? Lt

Army Form C. 2118.

WAR DIARY
or
INTELLIGENCE SUMMARY.
(Erase heading not required.)

30 DAC   Aug 1916

Place	Date	Hour	Summary of Events and Information	Remarks and references to Appendices
			Changes in Officers. July & Aug, 1916.	
	7.7.16		2nd Lieut. S. MOLYNEUX to be temp. Capt. from 25.1.16. to 21.3.16 whilst com'g section London HvyBty 3½	
			2/Lieut (Temp Lieut) C. CASBOLT to be temp. Capt. from 22.3.16 whilst com'g section DAC	do
	12.7.16		2/Lieut. J.D.BELL posted from 30 D.A.C. to 154 Bde R.F.A. under orders from today	
	18.7.16		2/Lieut. A. KAY 30 D.A.C. posted to V/30. Heavy Trench Mortar Batt's under orders effect. from 20.6.16.	
	"		2/Lieut. T.E. BATEMAN to 30 D.A.C. 13.7.16.	
	27.7.16		2/Lieut. S. MOLYNEUX to be Temp. Lieut	London Gaz 23.6.16
	1.8.16		Lieut. R.R. LAW posted to 30 D.A.C.	
	"		" K. GRAY " "	do
	14.8.16		2/Lieut. F. GILMORE 30 D.A.C. posted to V/30. T.M. Batt'y. Effect from today	
	29.8.16		Lieut A.W. EMBERSON posted to 5th Divisional Arty	
	"		2/Lieut G.E.K. BEMAND do	
	"		" B.B. ORMEROD do	
	"		" T.H. BRINDLE KELLY (att'd) do	

Signed Hugh F. Tombs
30/8/16.

Army Form C. 2118.

WAR DIARY
or
INTELLIGENCE SUMMARY.
(Erase heading not required.)

Instructions regarding War Diaries and Intelligence Summaries are contained in F.S. Regs., Part II. and the Staff Manual respectively. Title pages will be prepared in manuscript.

Place	Date	Hour	Summary of Events and Information	Remarks and references to Appendices
			Ammunition issued August 1916.	
			A. A×. B. B× B× (Pouches filled) S.A.A.	
	Week ending			
	6.8.16		232. — — 160. — —	
	13.8.16		3000 600. — 1208 — 145000	
	20.8.16		1713 4980 — 656 — 386000	
	27.8.16		4945 5580 — 2024 — 531000	
			This does not include ammunition drawn from 31st Div & 2nd Div 3 Section & issued to Regt groups.	

G.W. Huskisson Lt Col 12th DA

Vol 16

War Diary.
of
30th Divisional Ammunition Column
for September 1916.

Volume X

Army Form C. 2118.

September 1916   30th D.A.C.

WAR DIARY
or
~~INTELLIGENCE SUMMARY.~~
(Erase heading not required.)

Instructions regarding War Diaries and Intelligence Summaries are contained in F. S. Regs., Part II. and the Staff Manual respectively. Title pages will be prepared in manuscript.

Place	Date	Hour	Summary of Events and Information	Remarks and references to Appendices
BETHUNE	9.9.16		2nd Lieut C.F.TURNER appointed Adjutant with effect from 17.5.16	
"			2nd Lieut C.F.TURNER promoted to Lieut with effect from 17.5.16 on appointment as Adjutant	
BETHUNE	19.9.16	9 a.m.	Column moved from BETHUNE via CHOQUES, MARLES les MINES, ACHEUX, FLORINGHEM to MONCHY CAYEUX, PERNES, TANGRY, HESTRUS. A Weather very wet.	
MONCHY CAYEUX	21.9.16	8 a.m.	Column moved from MONCHY CAYEUX via WAVRANS, HERNICOURT, CROIX, CROISETTE, NUNCQ, LIGNY SUR CANCHE to VACQUERIE Weather wet in morning but clearing at midday	
VACQUERIE	22.9.16	7 a.m.	move from VACQUERIE via BONNIERES, BARLY, OCCOCHES, HEM, GEZAINCOURT to BEAUVAL. Weather dry + bright	
BEAUVAL	23.9.16	8 a.m.	move from BEAUVAL to TALMAS fine weather	
TALMAS	26.9.16	10 a.m.	move from TALMAS via RUBEMPRÉ, BEAUCOURT, BEHENCOURT, FRANVILLERS, ALBERT R.H. to point D.12 h.5.8. thence to DERNANCOURT. Column inspected in line of march at RUBEMPRÉ by MAJ. GEN. SHEA Com'g 30th Division. Weather fine	
DERNANCOURT	27.9.16		Column moved to position in the line. H.Q. at cross roads MEAULTE - FRICOURT. BRAY - ALBERT takes over Ammunition supply from 7th DAC 5 p.m. 2 sections S.A.A. with parties of 8 Echelon + 2 sections grenades of B Echelon New Zealand DAC attached to convoy unit supply of Ammunition	

Original Sept 1916.   30 D.A.C.

Army Form C. 2118.

WAR DIARY
or
INTELLIGENCE SUMMARY.
(Erase heading not required.)

Instructions regarding War Diaries and Intelligence Summaries are contained in F. S. Regs., Part II. and the Staff Manual respectively. Title pages will be prepared in manuscript.

Place	Date	Hour	Summary of Events and Information	Remarks and references to Appendices
BETHUNE	4.9.16		Changes in Officers	
	6.9.16		Lieut. J.G. Donnelly posted from A/149 to No 4 Section	
	"		2/Lt H.W. Hill posted from B/149 to No 2 Section 30 D.A.C.	
	"		Lt J.G. Donelly " from A/149 to No 4 Section 30 D.A.C.	
	"		2/Lt F.W. Walker " " 5/149 to No 4 " "	
	"		2/Lt P.R. Winser " " C/157 to No. 3. " "	
	"		Capt A Dalgleish " DAC to A/149.	
	"		Capt F Noakes attd 30 DAC to No 3 Sect until posted from 5th inor.	
	31.9.16		Lieut A W Emberson posted from 30 DAC to 5th Div Arty.	
			2/Lt G.E. Bemand " " " " " "	
			" B.B. Ormarod " " " " " "	
			" T.H Brindle Kelly " " " " " "	

J.W. Wembley Lt Col
3. O.D.A.C.
Com. 5.10.16

Vol II

War Diary
of
30 Divisional Ammunition Column
for
October 1916.

VOLUME XI.

original 30 D.A.C.

WAR DIARY
or
INTELLIGENCE SUMMARY

Army Form C. 2118.

October 1916

(Erase heading not required.)

Place	Date	Hour	Summary of Events and Information	Remarks and references to Appendices
F.6.C.3.9	9.10.16		A. Echelon moved to position on MAMETZ – MONTAUBAN Road. S.26.C.9.d. Section affiliated to Brigades. No.1 & 145th, No.2 & 149th, No.3 & 150th to assist wagon lines supply of ammunition to gun positions	J.P.S.W.
"	11.10.16		B. Echelon supplying ammunition to gun positions. 62nd Brigade coming to wrd position to take up wagon. Ammunition carried by pack	J.P.S.W.
S.26.C	12.10.16		Headquarters removed to MAMETZ – MONTAUBAN Road S.26.C. – A Echelon moved with Battery wagon lines to position North of MONTAUBAN =	J.P.S.W.
"	13.10.16		B Echelon moved to position vacated by 148 Bde on MAMETZ – MONTAUBAN Rd	J.P.S.W.
"	15.10.16		A Echelon moves to S.28.C. (No 3 Section) & S.22.C. (1 & 2 Sections) for convenience in receiving Battery wagon lines –	J.P.S.W.
	21.10.16		No.1 & 2 Sections' horse lines shelled – 2 wagons destroyed – no casualties. Move to S.26.C. & Sadlers making packs for convenience in taking up ammunition. Zackets replaced for wagons	J.P.S.W.
MONTAUBAN	30.10.16		Ammunition dump taken over from 41st D.A.C. at St MOLYNEUX and in charge	J.P.S.W.
	28.10.16		Several 5.9" H.S. shells burst in the lines occupied by No 2 Section during	J.P.S.W.

Army Form C. 2118.

WAR DIARY
or
INTELLIGENCE SUMMARY.
(Erase heading not required.)

Instructions regarding War Diaries and Intelligence Summaries are contained in F. S. Regs., Part II. and the Staff Manual respectively. Title pages will be prepared in manuscript.

Place	Date	Hour	Summary of Events and Information	Remarks and references to Appendices
			the night. One falling at the foot of the flagstaff. No casualties or damage. the shells bursting in deep mud appear to have very little effect.	

J M Wheatley
Lt. 701.1st Sqd
Comm? 3rd D.A.C.
31.10.16.

T2134. Wt. W708—776. 500000. 4/15. Sir J. C. & S.

Army Form C. 2118.

30th D.A.C.

WAR DIARY
or
INTELLIGENCE SUMMARY.

(Erase heading not required.)

Instructions regarding War Diaries and Intelligence Summaries are contained in F. S. Regs., Part II. and the Staff Manual respectively. Title pages will be prepared in manuscript.

Place	Date	Hour	Summary of Events and Information						Remarks and references to Appendices

Ammunition issued by Column during October 1916.

Week ending	A.	Ax.	B.	Bx.	Ox. Gas.	S.A.A.
Oct. 7	17.705	5.393	—	6.435	150.	249.000
" 14	18.818	12.850	—	7.906	914.	3.000
" 21	14.249	7.275	—	6.002	150.	—
" 25	958	1.400	—	320	—	—
" 25 & 31	2.152	3.319	—	818	—	—
	53.882	30.237	—	21.484	1.214	252.000

In addition to the above the teams belonging to A Echelon have drawn ammunition direct on behalf of the Battery wagon lines & carried it to the gun positions.

W.D. Wheatley
Lt. Col. R.F.A.

November 1916. WAR DIARY or INTELLIGENCE SUMMARY.

Army Form C. 2118.

30. D.A.C.
Vol 12

Place	Date	Hour	Summary of Events and Information	Remarks and references to Appendices
MONTAUBAN	1.11.16		Attached to 2. Australian Division 1st ANZAC Corps	JMM
"	16.11.16		No 1 & 3 Sections relieved by 1 & 3 Sections 1st Australian D.A.C. marched to K area MORLANCOURT - Mud very deep everywhere -	JMM
"	17.11.16		MORLANCOURT - No 2 Section, H.Q. & wagon lines struggled on through enemy aeroplane & hostile attempts. Weather frosty, some snow. Billet by road. 1 & 3 Section marched to BUSSY.	JMM
"	18.11.16		Remainder of D.A.C. relieved by 1st Australian D.A.C. marched to K area	JMM
MORLANCOURT	18.11.16		weather very wet - march difficult owing to mud & congestion of traffic. Route via CARNOY. MEAULTE - Lantie - H.Q.. No 2 Section & B Echelon march to Bonnay - via VILLE BUIRE -	JMM
BONNAY.	19.11.16		HEILLY. - Billets - fair	JMM
TALMAS	20.11.16		Column march to TALMAS - via LANEUVILLE - GUÉRRIEUX. Coisy Village BRIAGE. weather fine. Roads bad at first - improved later	JMM
MILLY.	21.11.16		Column march to MILLY via BEAUQUESNE. DOULLENS - Roads good weather fine - Billets poor - leave reopened.	JMM
	23.11.16		B Echelon moved to BAVINCOURT to relieve 46th Div	JMM
	24.11.16		Reserve Park - A Echelon resting. Rain.	JMM

WAR DIARY
or
INTELLIGENCE SUMMARY.

Army Form C. 2118.

30 D.A.C.

November 1916

Place	Date	Hour	Summary of Events and Information	Remarks and references to Appendices
Montauban	31/10/16		Changes in Officers — 2/Lieut. S.S. Evans from 30 DAC to A/145. " E Barker from attached 30 DAC to No 1 Sect.	
	23/11/16		Lieut. W.P. Fitzgerald from 2/30 T.M.Batt to 30 DAC	

Army Form C. 2118.

WAR DIARY
or
INTELLIGENCE SUMMARY.
(Erase heading not required.)

Place	Date	Hour	Summary of Events and Information	Remarks and references to Appendices
	Week ending		Ammunition issued by Column. Nov 1916.	
			A AX BX 4.5" Gas	
	7.11.16		26518 14706 9308 —	
	14.11.16		22996 8630 6816 300	
	15/16, 19/11/16		12218 6134 3658 —	
			61732 29670 19782 300	

G.W. Mackay Major R.F.A.
Lieut Col. 2/2 R.C
Comm. 1.12.16

WAR DIARY or INTELLIGENCE SUMMARY

Army Form C. 2118.

30th D.A.C.
1st December

Place	Date	Hour	Summary of Events and Information	Remarks and references to Appendices
SAULTY	2.12.16		H.Q. & A Echelon move to forward area. — H.Q. & No 3 Sections to SAULTY. No 2 Section to COULLEMONT. — Haynets of horses on standing already prepared. No lines cover. — Some standings to enable men & horses to be under cover.	Cx
"	13.12.16	3pm	SAULTY – LARBRET Station shelled during unloading of Remount – Ammunition Standard footfall removed – no Casualties	C3
			4. 5 inch Howitzer Ammunition Wagons complete turnout for A Echelon. 8th F.S. Wagons complete turnout for B Echelon attached to to ammunition taken over on issuance of an additional Howitzer Battery in 30th Divisional Artillery, namely the 394th Howitzer Battery (now C" Battery 150 (Bde)	Cx
	21.12.16		CAPT. H NOAKES posted from No 3 Section to command B Echelon from L2 Section to command No 3 Section to embark. — LIEUT. H.GRAY from B Echelon to charge of Ammunition Dump. CAPT H HIGGINS	Cx

Gun Ammunition issued by Column during December
Week ending 7.12.16   172 rds A   36 rds Ax   4490 rds B
15.12.16   2020   4638   4320
22.12.16   1196   322   540
31.12.16   420   1472   2436

Vol 14

WAR DIARY
OF
30th D.A.C.
for
January 1917
Volume XIV
Dec 1918

WAR DIARY

Army Form C. 2118.

30th D.A.C.

INTELLIGENCE SUMMARY for December.
(Erase heading not required.)

Place	Date	Hour	Summary of Events and Information	Remarks and references to Appendices
SAULTY	2.12.16		H.Q. & 'A' Echelon move to forward area. - H.Q. 1 & 3 Sections to SAULTY No 2 Section to COULLEMONT. - Majority of horses on standings already prepared with head covers - Some standings (but complete - men billeted) Gun Park	CJ
"	13.12.16	5 pm	SAULTY - LARBRET Station shelled during unloading of Remounts - animals stampeded but all returned - no casualties. 4.5 inch Howitzer Ammunition Wagons complete turnout for 'A' Echelon, 4 & 5 Wagons complete turnout for 'B' Echelon, attached to 46 Division taken over on arrival of an additional Howitzer Battery in 30th Divisional Artillery namely the 374 Howitzer Battery (now "C" Battery 150 Bde.)	CJ
"	21.12.16		CAPT. H. NOAKES. posted from No. 3 Section to Command 'B' Echelon. LIEUT. H. GRAY from No. 2 Section to Command No. 3 Section temporarily. CAPT. H. WILKINS from 'B' Echelon to charge of Ammunition dump.	CJ
			Gun Ammunition issued by Column during December	CJ

Week ending	18 pr. A.	172 pr. A.	4.5 in. Ar.	60 pr. Bx.	
7.12.16			463½	490	
15.12.16	2020			4320	
22.12.16	1196		232½	540	
29.12.16	460		1472	245½	

C.J. Murray Lt RFA
Adjt. for O.C. 30 D.A.C.
(absent on leave)

Army Form C. 2118.

30 D.A.C.

WAR DIARY
or
INTELLIGENCE SUMMARY.
(Erase heading not required.)

Jan. 1917.

Place	Date	Hour	Summary of Events and Information	Remarks and references to Appendices
SAVLTY.	1.1.17		Reorganization of Field Artillery. The D.A.C. in future consists of A Echelon of 2 Sections only & B Echelon slightly reduced. The present 1 & 2 Sections are retained, each increased to correspond with the increase of Horse Batteries in the affiliated Brigades from 6 to 6 horses. Each Section is moved of 1 Subaltern, 1 Sergeant, 3 Artificers, 31 Rank & File (Total 36), 3 Riding & 24 draught horses. The late No 3 Section becomes 150th Army Field Artillery Brigade Gun Column.	30 Div Art⁵ 2/732
	4.1.17		Honours & rewards. Mentioned in Despatches. Lieut C.F. TURNER. 30 D.A.C. 58124. Serg⁺ (A.C.) S.A FLAXMAN. 30 D.A.C.	London Gazette Jan 4 '17 21.1.17
"	8.1.17		These are the first honours that have been awarded to this Column. 2/Lieut H.E.M. FOX from 30 D.A.C. to 149 Bde R.F.A. 2/L⁺ H.A.NOMAN to 149 Bde R.F.A.	
"	13.1.17		H.Q. D.A.C. & A. ECHELON relieved by 49th D.A.C. Marched to MILLY & later over billet returning. Owing to outbreak of mange being horses of 49th D.A.C. principal standings are out of bounds. Very cramped standings on 2 road - poor billets. Very little accommodation available.	
MILLY				

Army Form C. 2118.

WAR DIARY
or
INTELLIGENCE SUMMARY.
(Erase heading not required.)

Instructions regarding War Diaries and Intelligence Summaries are contained in F. S. Regs., Part II. and the Staff Manual respectively. Title pages will be prepared in manuscript.

Place	Date	Hour	Summary of Events and Information	Remarks and references to Appendices
MILLY	15/1/17		B. Echelon relieved at BAVINCOURT by B. Echelon 49 D.A.C. moved via LUCHEUX to GROUCHES.	
"	17/1/17		Column fatigues recommence. 15 wagons to BEAUVOIS for oats and straw for distribution to Brigades. 20 wagons daily to LUCHEUX FOREST for drawing for horse standings	
"	20/1/17		Two wagons per Battery & 1 per Brigade H.Q. sent to Column to form Battence & proceed to BAC DU NORD to assist with ammunition supply to guns	
"	29/1/17	10 a.m.	Column inspected & marching order by G.O.C.R.A.	
"	31/1/17		Column moves to GOUY-EN-ARTOIS. hopeless journey through LUCHEUX by G.R. Division. Hard frost & fall of snow during night caused severe supply a dangerous hitch delay on road. Relieved 14 DAC-Route via LUCHEUX HUMBERCOURT. COULLEMONT. SAULTY BAVINCOURT	

Army Form C. 2118.

WAR DIARY
or
INTELLIGENCE SUMMARY.
(Erase heading not required.)

Place	Date	Hour	Summary of Events and Information	Remarks and references to Appendices
			Changes in Officers Jan 1917	
	8.1.17		2/Lt H.F.M. Fox from 30 DAC to 149 B/55 R.F.A	
			2/Lt H.A. Mohan " " 145 "	
	22.1.17		Capt H. Wilkins " 30 D.A.C to England 21.1.17 Authy A.G. GHQ No D/266 dated 15.1.17	
			2/Lt F. Barker " 30 DAC to 20th Divl Arty 24.1.17 Auth A.G. GHQ No D/1104/1000 date 10.1.17	
	26.1.17		2/Lt E.J. Halliwell having joined the 30th Divl Arty 25.1.17 posted to 30 DAC	
			2/Lt E.J. Halliwell from 30 DAC Proceed to A/149 Bde R.F.A 26.1.17	
	29.1.17		Lt W. Brunwell from 36 D.A (Supern) to 30 DAC	
Mecknes	7.1.17		Gun Ammunition supplied January 1917	
			A× B×	
			£ 600 760 604	
			554 298 911	
	13.1.17		1354 1758 1515	
			Column 1 obtained 1 consignment of Ammunition from reserve at 20 DAC 13.1.17 [signature]	

Vol 15

War Diary
of
30th Divisional Ammunition
Column
for
February 1917
Volume XV

WAR DIARY or INTELLIGENCE SUMMARY

Army Form C. 2118.

30 DAC

February 1917

Place	Date	Hour	Summary of Events and Information	Remarks and references to Appendices
GOUY en ARTOIS			From the middle of January to the middle of February there was a very severe frost, accompanied by falls of snow at the outset. The cold was severer & more prolonged than has been recorded for this part of France for upwards of 20 years. During this period the admonishing of our horses in the ordinary manner has been from 1 day but on the thaw after the middle of the month they have been extremely muddy. No prepared standing exists in the villages. During these weeks the wagons of B Echelon have been engaged daily in carrying supplies for the Divisional Train, & those of A Echelon Engineers stores to AGNY & ACHICOURT. Ammunition has not been required in large quantities. After the breaking of the frost in the middle of the month "thaw resolutions" after the breaking up of the roads by heavy traffic came into force (entry) till the end of the month. In spite of these restrictions the Column was still called upon to do a large amount of work. Motor losses not having allowed to use the roads	

Army Form C. 2118.

WAR DIARY
or
INTELLIGENCE SUMMARY.
(Erase heading not required.)

Place	Date	Hour	Summary of Events and Information	Remarks and references to Appendices
			The column had to provide transport to carry the Brigade train with supplies, & considerable quantities of Engineers stores & grenades & had still to be sent up to the line to meet urgent requirements	

Ammunition & Grenades issued Feb 1917

	A.	A X.	B X.	S.A.A.	GRENADES			T.N. BOMBS		PISTOL WEBLEY
					Mills	20	23	2"	3" Stokes	
Week ending Feb. 7,	2346.	1243	754	—	—	—	—	—	—	—
" 14	369	912	720	59,000	1008	—	408	—	—	5320
" 21	—	806	120	116,000	3192	800	492	—	399	2064
" 28	—	636	—	140,650	10296	—	4140	200	720	6204
	2715	3597	1594	315,650	14496	800	5040	200	1099	13755
							5840			

MW Hawley Lt Col
L.E. Corp

Army Form C. 2118.

WAR DIARY
or
INTELLIGENCE SUMMARY.
(Erase heading not required.)

30th D.A.C.
March 1917

Place	Date	Hour	Summary of Events and Information	Remarks and references to Appendices
GOUY-EN-ARTOIS			During the first half of the month "horse rotations" have been in force limiting the use of lly roads to horse transport for supplies only. 0 about the 11th around 3 ram 30 G.S. Wagons from B Echelon were detailed daily to draw supplies from Lattre) to Pelving point. Ammunition lorries limited to those of urgent necessity.	CA.
	12.3.17		A.P.P. transferred from No. 6 (Cavalry) Amm. Sub-park to No. 1. Dump	CA.
			Govy - lorries begun to draw 20mm rds for Guns 18pr. (Not stow 30 of A.S.A.P.) and 14 DD rds for 4.5 How at Gun positions	CX. CA.
	16.3.17		Column moved from Gouy to Point G.20.d. (Map Sheet 57C.) Camb. 500 yards W. of MONCHIET - Horses picketed in shelter men in lean-to huts. Owing to bad condition of roads many of them are entirely close to traffic, the	CA.
MONCHIET			greatest difficulty is being experienced in sending convoys forward.	CA.
	19.3.17		Orders to reconnoitre WAILLY for Site for Ammunition dump & Camp for Column	CA.
MONCHIET	21.3.17		Orders to reconnoitre BRETENCOURT for Sites - dumps formed at SUGAR.	CA.
			FACTORY. R.27.b.9.9.	CA.
	22.3.17		No. 1. Section moved to SUGAR FACTORY, BRETENCOURT. Orders to reconnoitre for	CA.

Army Form C. 2118.

WAR DIARY
or
INTELLIGENCE SUMMARY.
(Erase heading not required.)

30th D.A.C.
March 1917 Vol 6

Place	Date	Hour	Summary of Events and Information	Remarks and references to Appendices
GOUY-EN-ARTOIS			During the first half of the month "train restrictions" have been in force limiting the use of the roads by horse transport to supplies only. to avoid the Divisional train 30 gd Wagons from B Echelon were detailed daily to draw supplies from Railhead to Refilling Point. Ammunition lorries limited to these of urgent necessity.	(1)
	12.3.17		H.Q. 2 transferred from No. 6 (Orange) dump Senncourt to No. 1 (Lemon) Gouy. — were begun to dump 2000 rds per gun 18 Rdr (approx. 50 of A.4.18) and 1400 rds of 4.5 Howitzer at gun positions	(1) (1)
MONCHIET	16.3.17		Column moved from Gouy to front G.20.d. (map Sheet 51.c) — Camp 300 yards W. of Monchiet. — Horses (besides our Shetts) were in fair condition of trace in the condition of roads many of them are entirely unfit to traffic, and greatest difficulty is being experienced in sending convoys forward.	(1)
	19.3.17		Orders to reconnoitre Wailly to site of ammunition dump of Camp for Column	(1)
MONCHIET	20.3.17		Orders to reconnoitre BRETENCOURT for site — Advance parties at Sugar Factory R.27.c.9.9.	(1)
	22.3.17		No. 1 Section moved to Sugar Factory Bretencourt. Orders to reconnoitre for	(1)

Army Form C. 2118.

WAR DIARY
or
INTELLIGENCE SUMMARY.
(Erase heading not required.)

Instructions regarding War Diaries and Intelligence Summaries are contained in F. S. Regs, Part II. and the Staff Manual respectively. Title pages will be prepared in manuscript.

Place	Date	Hour	Summary of Events and Information	Remarks and references to Appendices
			Changes in Officers - March 1917	
	3.3.17		2nd Lieut. C.W. WARD joined 3rd D.A.C. Posted to A/148 Bde. R.F.A. 7.3.17.	
	6.3.17		" R.B. STEWART " " " " " B/149 "	
	"		" H. KAY " " " " " "	
	7.3.17		Lieut. H. ASQUITH " " " Posted to C/148 Bde R.F.A. 7.3.17	
	"		2nd Lieut. H.B. JEMMETT " " " " " A/149 "	
	16.3.17		" H. KNIGHT " " " "	
	"		" R.H. PEAKE " " " Posted to D/149 Bde R.F.A. 28.3.17	
	"		" C.G. JOHNSON " " " "	
	"		" E.C. CUMBERLIDGE " " " and reported to Base Depot. 19.3.17	
	24.3.17		Lieut. J.D. NEWSOM " " "	
	25.3.17		2nd Lieut. E.D. ETHERIDGE . " " "	
	28.3.17		Lt. Colonel J.P.D. WHEATLEY admitted to Hospital, proceeded later to 4th Divisional Artillery.	
	31.3.17		Lieut. S. MOLYNEUX posted to 4th Divisional Artillery.	O.C.

WAR DIARY or INTELLIGENCE SUMMARY

Army Form C. 2118.

Place	Date	Hour	Summary of Events and Information	Remarks and references to Appendices
			Changes in Officers - March 1917	
	3.3.17		2nd Lieut. C.W. WARD joined 2n DAC. Posted to A/148. Bde RFA 7.3.17	
	6.3.17		" R B STEWART " " " B/149 "	
			" H NAY " " " "	
	7.3.17		Lieut Lt ASQUITH " Posted to C/148 Bde RFA 7.3.17	
			2nd Lieut H.B. JEMMETT " A/149 "	
	18.3.17		" H. KNIGHT " " "	
			" R.H. PEAKE " Posted to D/149 Bde RFA 28.3.17	
			" C.G. JOHNSON " "	
			" E.C. CUMBERLIDGE " and returned to Base depot. 19.3.17	
	24.3.17		Lieut J.D. NEWSOM "	
	25.3.17		2nd Lieut E.D. ETHERIDGE "	
	28.3.17		Lt Colonel J.P.D WHEATLEY admitted to Stationary Hospital sick	C.T.
	31.3.17		Lieut S MOLYNEUX posted to 4th Divisional Artillery.	

(signed) H ...... RFA
A/ot/r O.C. 2. DAC

Army Form C. 2118.

WAR DIARY
or
INTELLIGENCE SUMMARY.
(Erase heading not required.)

Place	Date	Hour	Summary of Events and Information	Remarks and references to Appendices
BAILLEULVAL	23.3.17		Camp for Column at BAILLEULVAL. — Dumping of Ammunition at gun positions suspended. Nos 2 & 3 Sections Headquarters moved from MONCHIET to BAILLEULVAL. Men in billets & dugouts. Horses picketed on Stubble.	CJ.
	24.3.17		Another Ammunition dump formed at Point R.32.a.9.6. under L. Shoulderney.	CJ.
	28.3.17		Lt Col G.S.A. Wheatley met with an accident (fractured leg) whilst riding to No.1 Section. His horse stumbled & fell in RIVIERE.	CJ.
	30.3.17		Removal of all Ammunition from Govy. dump to dump at point R.32.a.9.8 completed. Lt. S. Anneville took over this dump & the Bruges loading dump from Lt Shoulderney.	CJ.
	31.3.17		Dumping of 1 m/m site for gun at new gun positions commenced. Lt Col G.S.A. Wheatley evacuated with fractured tibia.	CJ.

10 Haymes engaged on Campagnard notes
Ammunition issued during March 1917.

	A.	Ax.	Bx.	S.A.A.
Weeking ending 7th March	—	724	730.	962,000
14 "	9844	6686	3526	39,000
21 "	12140	10,252	3780	927,000
31 "	11,554	12,754	482	45,000
Total	33,538	32,536.	12,872.	1,972,000	CJ.

Army Form C. 2118.

WAR DIARY
or
INTELLIGENCE SUMMARY.
(Erase heading not required.)

Instructions regarding War Diaries and Intelligence Summaries are contained in F. S. Regs., Part II. and the Staff Manual respectively. Title pages will be prepared in manuscript.

Place	Date	Hour	Summary of Events and Information	Remarks and references to Appendices
BAILLEUVAL	23.3.17		Camp for Column at BAILLEUVAL. - Quartering of Ammunition at Gun Positions Suspended for 2 & 3 Sections. Headquarters moved from MONCHIET to BAILLEUVAL. Men in Billets & dugouts, horses picketed on stubble.	(A)
	24.3.17		Another Ammunition dump formed at Point R.32.a.9.6. under Lt. Shopyeng	(B)
	28.3.17		2nd Lt. J.P.O. Hurstly met with an Accident (fractured leg) whilst riding to No. 1 Section. He	(C)
			horse stumbled & fell in RIVIERE	
	30.3.17		Removal of all Ammunition from Gov't Dump to dumps at Point R.33.a.9.3. Cmblarus. 2nd Lt. J. Donnelly took over this dump & its Sugar Factory Dump from Lt. Montgomery.	(D)
	31.3.17		Dumping of 1000 rds. for gun at new Gun Position commenced. 2nd Lt. J.P.O. Hurstly evacuated with fractured tibia	(E)
			10 Wagons engaged in Carrying X.3 Metal	
			Ammunition issued during March 1917.	

	A	AX	BX	SAA
Week ending 7th March	-	724	720.	962,000
14 "	9844	8656.	3536.	39,000
21 "	12,140	10,252.	3780	927,000
31 "	11,554.	12,754.	4826.	45,000
Total	33,538	32,532.	12,872.	1,972,000 (F)

T2134. Wt. W708—776. 500000. 4/15. Sir J. C. & S.

Army Form C. 2118.

30 D.A.C.
April 1917

WAR DIARY
or
INTELLIGENCE SUMMARY.
(Erase heading not required.)

Place	Date	Hour	Summary of Events and Information	Remarks and references to Appendices
BAILLEULVAL	1.4.17		2nd Lieutenant C.G. JOHNSON posted to A/149 in exchange with 2nd Lieutenant H.B. JENNETT. Staff of O.R. arrived from Brae. Q.F. 18 Bde Wagon of M. Section exchanged for a damaged Wagon of A/148 Bde. Ammunition carried by Batteries. A.8288 AX 4680 BX 5260	
"	2.4.17		Sugar factory dump empties of Ammunition. Relief ordered to Brigades as 148 Bde. 6 O.R. ↓149 Bde. 23 O.R. Ammunition cars to Batteries. A.9378. AX 9575. BX 3960. Heavy fall of snow much difficulty experienced in getting Ammunition forward. 30 S. Wagons & 12 Heavy Wagons details to assist 160/153 Bde. in bringing the Ammunition forward.	
"	3.4.17		Ammunition cars to Batteries. AX 5476 BX 5246	
"	4.4.17		12 Wagons & 5 How. details to assist 153 Bde RFA to get Ammunition to Guns. Ammunition cars to Batteries. A 1944 AX 1576 BX 1468	
"	5.4.17		12 Wagons & 5 How. details to assist 153 RFA Bde to get Ammunition to Guns. 15 Sd. Wagons sent to Gun positions in CRINCHON VALLEY (M.>.d.6.2.) to return Ammunition which has to be left for Batteries going to forward	

WAR DIARY or INTELLIGENCE SUMMARY

Army Form C. 2118.

30 T.A.C. April 1917

Place	Date	Hour	Summary of Events and Information	Remarks and references to Appendices
BAILLEULVAL	1.4.17		2nd Lieutenant C.G. JOHNSON (late to 2/149) on exchange with 2/Lieutenant H.B. JENNETT. 2nd Lt. G. O.R. arrive from Base. Q.F. 18 h. Hagers of No. 1 Section exchanged (for a damage) Hagers of M/148 Bde Ammunition about By Batteries. A.8288 A.4680 B.5260 1 Sugar Tickets drawd. Subtotal of Ammunition.	
"	2.4.17		Recd [?] by Brigadier no. 1148 Bde. 6 O.R. 1/149 Bde 23 O.R. Ammunition ram by Batteries. A.9378. B.9515. B.3960. Heavy pull of Guns [?] difficulty [?] in getting Ammunition [?] 30. St. Georges M.S.R. ready [?] [?] much 168-333 due to Infantry. Ammunition [?]	
"	3.4.17		Ammunition ram by Batteries A.3432. B.2410. 12. Hagers 4.5 ins. Guns to travel 155 Bde RR to get Ammunition to Guns. Ammunition rams by Batteries. A.1700. B.1506. B.1468.	
"	4.4.17		13 Hagers 4.5 Guns to travel 155 H.F.A Bde to get Ammunition to Guns.	
"	5.4.17		15. G/2 Hagers sent to [?] firing Batteries in CRINCHON VALLEY (M.2 d.6.2) to [?] Ammunition [?] was to be left to Batteries more like France	

WAR DIARY or INTELLIGENCE SUMMARY

Army Form C. 2118.

Place	Date	Hour	Summary of Events and Information	Remarks and references to Appendices
BAILLEULVAL	5.4.17		10. S/S Hagons detailed to Cartage Store to Shrapnel Corner (R.H.d.) Ammunition issued to Batteries A.940. A.977. B× 1776.	
	6.4.17		15. S/S Hagons sent to return Ammunition from O.P. Gun Position 148. B× R×R Ammunition issued to Batteries. B× 960 Rds. Smoke Shells 4.5 How. 376.	
	7.4.17		4. Gunner Hagons sent to work under the Divisional Bombing Officer to proportion Gun & Rifle Grenades, attached to each Infantry Bgde. & with Ammunition between Infantry & two Divisional Bombing Officer. Ammunition issued to Batts. B× 728.	
	8.4.17		2nd Echelon Batty 15. V.R. Issued to Boulogne for Remount for Brigade. Ammunition issued to Batteries. A.6012. A.5608. B× 540.	
	9.4.17		Capt Sparrow R.A.M.C. MO & C. 30 C.F.A. arrived to assume dressing Station at 3 point S. 3. a 0.5. All Echelons full ready to move forward. Ammunition issued to Batteries. A 9326. A 8994. A (Smoke) 1000. B× 14500	
BAILLEULVAL	10.4.17		Nos. 1 & 2 Sections turned out at 7 a.m. to find grass which had moved forward. Ammunition issued to Batteries. A 2962. A 3864. B× 33000.	

Army Form C. 2118.

WAR DIARY
or
INTELLIGENCE SUMMARY.
(Erase heading not required.)

Place	Date	Hour	Summary of Events and Information	Remarks and references to Appendices
BAILLEULVAL	5.4.17		10. Lt Hagona moved to Cushing Stores (R.H.A.) Ammunition issued to 2/3 Bttx. A.940. A.900. B x 1776. Smoke Shells 4.5 How 326. 15. Lt Hagona sent to return Ammunition from old gun positions 148.B x 5m. Ammunition issued to Batteries B x 960 rds.	
	6.4.17		4. Smoke Hagona sent forward under the Divisional Bombing officer. Not successful. 2/1st N.Z. Orders Atrbuted to each Infantry Bde. for order Ammunition between infantry Bde & Divisional Dumps. Ammunition issued to Batts. B x 72.	
	7.4.17		2nd Lt Tatlin Ibrotts 15. D.A. Ammunition to Batteries for Barrage for Renewal for Brigades. Ammunition issued to Batteries. A.6012. A R 5508. B x 540. Capt Sherson Leaves. H.Q. 4 N.Z. to 31st D.A.C. Stores to Division Ammunition Stations allotted. S. 3. a D.5.	
	8.4.17		All Batteries full ready to move forward. Ammunition issued to Batteries. A.6336. A.8994. A (Smoke) 1000. B x 1400.	
BAILLEULVAL	10.4.17		Nos 1 & 2. Sections issued orders from to gun Waggon lines had moved forward Ammunition issued to Batteries. A 2962. A R 3364. B x 33 rds.	

Army Form C. 2118.

WAR DIARY
or
INTELLIGENCE SUMMARY.
(Erase heading not required.)

Instructions regarding War Diaries and Intelligence Summaries are contained in F. S. Regs., Part II. and the Staff Manual respectively. Title pages will be prepared in manuscript.

Place	Date	Hour	Summary of Events and Information	Remarks and references to Appendices
BAILLEULVAL	10.4.17		Lt. Gardener, 2nd Lt. Wright & 2nd Lt. E.O. Ethridge posted to 749 Bde.	
BAILLEULVAL S.2.b.8.3.	10.4.17		Advance Dumps established at Brickfields at point S.2.b.8.3.	
	11.4.17		No.1 Section moved from Sugar factory at Bavincourt R.27.b.9.9. to Brickfields. Column Headquarters moved from BAILLEULVAL to Brickfields S.2.b.8.3.	
			No.2 Section from BAILLEULVAL to Sugar factory R.27.b.9.9. B. Echelon from BAILLEULVAL to FERMONT. [French troops personnel] accompany B Echelon to FERMONT.	
S.2.b.8.3.			Ammunition issued to Batteries. A.3996. A.X.132. B.X.1444	
	12.4.17		Ammunition issued to Batteries A.1412. A.X.1624 B.X.284	
	13.4.17		Remainder BOISLEUX-AU-MONT for Battalion for 149 & two 1 & 2 Sections. Ammunition issued to Batteries - NIL	
BOISLEUX-AU-MONT.	14.4.17		Headquarters & A Echelon (less horse) to BOISLEUX-AU-MONT. S.10.d.5.5. Sheet 51h. Staff 1 officer & 11 O.R. joined from Base. 2nd Lt. V.J. GALLIE posted to No.2 Section. B ½ Echelon moved from FERMONT to Brickfields S.2.b.8.3.	
	15.4.17		Sergeant Artillery Clerk S. FLAXMAN posted to VII Corps as Chief Clerk A.2368. Ammunition returned to Battalion A.2368. A.X.2368. B.X.1576. 8 O.R. posted to 749 Bde R.F.A. as reinforcements	

WAR DIARY
or
INTELLIGENCE SUMMARY.
(Erase heading not required.)

Army Form C. 2118.

Place	Date	Hour	Summary of Events and Information	Remarks and references to Appendices
BAILLEULVAL	10.4.17		Lt J.A. Henson 2nd Lt Knight & 2nd Lt E.O. Etheridge joined to 149 Bde.	
BAILLEULVAL S.2.b.8.3	10.4.17		A Service Dump established at Brickfields at point S.2.b.8.3.	
	11.4.17		No.1. Section moved from Sugar factory at point R.27.b.9.9 L. Brickfield. Column Headquarters from BAILLEUVAL to Brickfield S.2.b.8.3. No 2 Section from BAILLEULVAL to Sugar factory. R.27.b.9.9. B. Echelon from BAILLEUVAL to FERMONT. French troops removed accompanying B Echelon to FERMONT.	
S.2.b.8.3.			Ammunition issued to Batteries A.3996. B.3152. Bx 1444 Ammunition issued to Batteries A.1412. Ax 1624 Bx 284	
	12.4.17		Bermuda BOISLEUX - AU - MONT. for batteries for 149 when 1 & 2 Section Ammunition issued to Batteries - NJ	
	13.4.17			
BOISLEUX - AU - MONT.	14.4.17		Headquarters of A. Echelon moved to BOISLEUX-AU-MONT. S.10.d.5.5. Short 3/4. Draft 1 Officer & 24. OR joined from Base 2nd Lt V.J. GALLIE joined to No 2 Section. B. Echelon moved from FERMONT to Brickfield S.2.b.8.3.	
	15.4.17		Sergeant Turner CMA. S FLAXMAN bar to VII Corps as Chief Clerk Ammunition issued to Batteries A.2368 Ax 2368 Bx 1376. S. O. R. Joined Lousy 3de RFA as reinforcements	

WAR DIARY or INTELLIGENCE SUMMARY

Army Form C. 2118.

Place	Date	Hour	Summary of Events and Information	Remarks and references to Appendices
BOILEUX-AU-MONT	16.4.17		2nd Lt. E.G. CUMBERLIDGE rejoins from Base. Q.F. Wagons of A Echelon filled with Ammunition from 20 Battery position at point S.6 d. & d. delivered same at new gun position.	
"	17.4.17		2nd Lt Cooke & party of 20 men with saddery Bickering gear proceeded to BOULOGNE for to Remounts. Q.F. Wagons of A Echelon carried out same detail of Ammunition as yesterday.	
"	18.4.17		Lt Colonel Hon. F.F. STANLEY. C.M.G. R.F.A. joins & resumes Command of the Column today. Q.F. Wagons of A Echelon carried out same detail of Ammunition as yesterday. Information received from 3rd Echelon that Lt. Colonel Jn. A. Wheatley evacuated to England on 8.4.17 per H.S. Stad Antwerpen suffering from pleurisy, Ichia and fibula.	
"	19.4.17		Reconnoitred new position for A Echelon at M.33.a.1.11 & M.33.a.2.8. on Houts new three will have to go a long way for it. Lieut G.H.TAYLOR joins from Base & sent to 750 Bac R.F.A.	

Army Form C. 2118.

WAR DIARY
or
INTELLIGENCE SUMMARY.
(Erase heading not required.)

Instructions regarding War Diaries and Intelligence Summaries are contained in F. S. Regs., Part II. and the Staff Manual respectively. Title pages will be prepared in manuscript.

Place	Date	Hour	Summary of Events and Information	Remarks and references to Appendices
BOILEUX - AU - MONT	16.4.17		2nd Lt E.G. CUMBERLIDGE returned from Base. O.F. Wagons of A Echelon of the first Ammunition Sub Sect S.C. & A.A. delivered same at new gun position.	
	17.4.17		2nd Coy ready & 3rd now out ready fetching gun position to BOULOGNE for 60 Rounds. O.F. Wagons of A Echelon carried out same detail of Ammunition as yesterday.	
	18.4.17		Lt Col Cyril Hon: S.F. STANLEY. C.M.G. R.F.A. DSO assumed Command of the Division to-day. O.F. Wagons of A Echelon carried out same detail of Ammunition as yesterday. H. Kingston returned from 3rd Echelon. That Lt Clow of A Bde also on leave. Lt England on 6.4.17 Lt. H.F. Snow tendered resigning from position (as) p/mr (Remounts) new position for A Echelon at M.33.a.1.11 & M.33.a.2.8. as does. new Harman Will have Forge a long way fr it. Lieut G.H. TAYLOR joined from Base at Isst Le No 150 Base Res.	

Army Form C. 2118.

WAR DIARY
or
INTELLIGENCE SUMMARY.
(Erase heading not required.)

Instructions regarding War Diaries and Intelligence Summaries are contained in F. S. Regs, Part II. and the Staff Manual respectively. Title pages will be prepared in manuscript.

Place	Date	Hour	Summary of Events and Information	Remarks and references to Appendices
BOISLEUX- AU- NONT	19.4.17		2nd Lieut N.L.L. Palmer joined from Base Depots to B. Echelon	
	20.4.17		2nd Lieut G REED joined from Base Depots to no 2 Section 30 DAC Ammunition supplied to Batteries A 3d. No 9344 Bx 13332 Guns moved to new positions at T.4.C & T.3.b Sheet 51.b. S.W. - QF Wagon A.E. Echelon assisting Batteries to get their Ammunition to their positions from their positions.	
"	21.4.17		Lieut H. Grey with party of 35 men carrying sandbags blankets few forward to BOULOGNE to draw portements. Enemy on Pattimpting to Shell the Railway dropped several Shells in & around the Wagon Lines of No.2. Section 1.4. S.A.G - no damage. was done.	
	22.4.17		A. E. Echelon delivering Ammunition Wg Sun. A.3488. Ar 1966. Bx 15 Fr. 2 pdr. Stokes ammn) with 58 Remounts for BOULOGNE - 2 having to be returned en route. - the 58 Remounts were handed on to Wag Rdg Res.	
	23.4.17		Enemy continued to Shell. Railway near our Wagon Lines - no damage. Heavy fighting in progress - Urgent appeals for Ammunition from Batteries but by turning out every Vehicle in the Column - delivered at Gun positions.	

WAR DIARY or INTELLIGENCE SUMMARY

Army Form C. 2118.

Place	Date	Hour	Summary of Events and Information	Remarks and references to Appendices
BOISLEUX-AU-MONT	19.4.17		2nd Lieut N.L.L. Palmer joined from Base Depot to B Echelon	
	20.4.17		2nd Lieut G REED joined from Base Depot to No 2 Section 30 NFC. Ammunition supplies to Batteries A 300 A/3344 B/1332. Guns now in position at T.4.c & T.3.b. Sheet 51.C. SW. QF Hagen A Echelon covers Battery brought their Ammunition bottom sections from above position	
"	21.4.17		2nd Lieut H Gray with body of 35 men Convoying Saddlery Limbers &c. proceeds to BOULOGNE to draw 70 Remounts. Enemy in Railway dug-outs sent Shells on & around the Hagen Area. No 1, No 2, Section H.Q.D. – no damage, wire down.	
	22.4.17		No 3 Echelon delivering Ammunition the Guns. A.3488. Ar.1966. B.1532. 2nd Lt. (Later Lieut) with 55 Remounts from BOULOGNE – changed horse wounded en route. – the 55 Remounts were handed in to Arty Bde RM. Enemy continues to shell Railway men and Hagen Area – no damage. Severe fighting in progress – Urgent appeals for Ammunition from Batteries met by drawing out more Vehicles in the Echelons – delivered at Gun positions	
	23.4.17			

WAR DIARY
or
INTELLIGENCE SUMMARY.
(Erase heading not required.)

Army Form C. 2118.

Place	Date	Hour	Summary of Events and Information	Remarks and references to Appendices
BOISLEUX- AU - MONT.	23.4.17		A. 6872 A.x 6034 B.x 4954. Hostile Shelling of Railway Continues - no damage	
	24.4.17		A & B echelon continues to supply ammunition to guns. Enemy shelled Railway - no damage	
"	25.4.17		Ammunition received by Batteries A. 3744 D.R 3974 B.R 2296.	
"	26.4.17		" " " A 735 A x 2397.	
			A Party from No. 1 Section 30 O.R. under 2nd Lieut. Howard, left Boise 0.25' a Central Sheet 51 b and returned a German light field Gun of 77 m.m. Calibre with several rounds of ammunition of various primary nature. - the Gun was quite new, bearing the date March 1917 - gun complete in every respect with the exception of sights, firing mechanism - the ammunition bore the same date as that on the Gun - it would appear that the Gun was used by the enemy in Anti- tank purposes Lt H. Gray returned from BOULOGNE with 70 Remount Horses & distributed to Batteries	
"	27.4.17		B Echelon returned from O.75 Central, New Heavy and New Medium	

WAR DIARY or INTELLIGENCE SUMMARY

Army Form C. 2118.

Place	Date	Hour	Summary of Events and Information	Remarks and references to Appendices
BOISLEUX-AU-MONT	23.4.17		A.6872 A.6324 B.4954. Heavy shelling of Ronsoy Continues - no damage.	
"	24.4.17		At 8 d.dh.n Enemy batteries located by Formosa to fire Enemy Shells Registered - no damage. Ammunition received L. Battery A.3744 A.39... B. 2296.	
"	25.4.17		A.3744 A.39... B. 2397 A. 735 B. 2397	
"	26.4.17		A patrol from No.1 Section 3... made 2nd ... improved Left ... O.25. a central shot 57 L and Registers a German light gun of 77 m.m Calibre with several rounds of Ammunition of gunning battery notice. - the gun was quite new having startup mark 1917-arms Complete in every respect with the exception of sights, spring Mechanism, the Commutator lens the same dots and shutters on the gun. It works appear that the gun was used by the enemy for Anti-Tank purposes. Lt Hargey returned from BOULOGNE with 70 Rounds of the same ... destroyed. L. Battery.	
"	27.4.17		3 Schlein Shells from O.25 exited Boisleux au Mont Mahieu	

T2134. Wt. W708-776. 500000. 4/15. Sir J. C. & S.

WAR DIARY
or
INTELLIGENCE SUMMARY of 3. D.A.C.

Army Form C. 2118.

Place	Date	Hour	Summary of Events and Information	Remarks and references to Appendices
BOISLEUX-AU-MONT	27.4.17		German minenwerfer Ammunition issued. A×532 B×1,146.	
"	28.4.17		Deliveries to D/148 & D/149 340 & 180 rounds B.C.BR for Special operation. 1,180 A. 1,216 B× & 360 B× issued to Batteries.	
"	29.4.17		2nd Lts C.D.HALL, E.G. EDNEY-HAYTER, and R.S. ELLISON & 1 Gunner Sgt. and 2 Wheelers from Base. A 504 B× 304 B×696 issued to Batteries.	
"	30.4.17		Wagon liner B. Echelon Shields - no Casualties. Ammunition issued A.1564 A×1164. B×816. Deliveries at Gun Positions of D/148 & D/149 B×m 286 & 164 rounds B.S.K respectively for Special Operations. Column Stars under orders of 18th Division Artillery from noon today.	

O. Khartr
Comdg 30 D.A.C. R.F.A.

Lt Colonel R.F.A.

1st May 1917.

WAR DIARY
or
INTELLIGENCE SUMMARY

Army Form C. 2118.

Place	Date	Hour	Summary of Events and Information	Remarks and references to Appendices
BOISLEUX-AU-MONT	27.4.17		German ammunition stopped. Ammunition issued: A×532, B×1146	
	28.4.17		Issued to 2/148 + 2/149 240 + 180 rounds B.C.B.R. for shrapnel shoots. 1180 A 136 HR + 360 J.S. rounds for Batteries. 2nd Lts C.D. HALL, E.G. EDNEY-HAYTER, and R.S. ELLISON + 1 farrier Sgt and	
	29.4.17		2 Shoeing Smiths from Base. A 504, HR 304, B×696 rounds to Batteries. B.S. Column Shells to Batteries.	
	30.4.17		Wagon lines A 155 + HR 1164 B× 816. Ammunition issued: L 148 + 2/149 Bdes 286 + 164 rounds Bdes at Gun positions for shrapnel shoots. B.S.R. distributed. Graze Shells under orders of 18th Division Artillery from from today.	
BOISLEUX-AU-MONT				

10 May 1917.

[signature]
Lieut. Col. RA
Comdg. 30 A.F.A. B.P.

Army Form C. 2118.

WAR DIARY
or
INTELLIGENCE SUMMARY. of 30. D.A.C.
(Erase heading not required.)

May 1917

Place	Date	Hour	Summary of Events and Information	Remarks and references to Appendices
BOISLEUX AU-MONT	1.V.17		The Guns of 148 Bde were moved forward about 700 yards and 24 O.F. Wagons of No.1 Section were detailed in consequence to assist in moving forward the ammunition for these Guns. Ammunition issued to Batteries 544 A. 544 B x 450 B x.	
"	2.V.17		Reconnoitred HENIN-SUR-COJEUL to Select Site for new forward Ammunition Dump – Position selected at point N.32.a Central Sheet 51.b. Orders received to carry on at Bucquoy dump pending further instructions Ammunition issued to Batteries A.488. Ax 1122 Bx 576	
"	3.V.17		Ammunition at Bucquoy dump exhausted & Sections had to proceed to NEUVILLE-VITASSE and BEAURAINS to refill Ammunition issued to Batteries A.7200 Ax 4592 Bx 2810.	
"	4.V.17		No Ammunition on dump or in Echelons – Arrangement made with 78th Division and under their Orders Batteries draw Ammunition from 18 O.F.C. dumps to complete dumps at same up to 500 rounds per Gun and full Echelons. Ammunition drawn from 18 O.F.C. A 3380 Ax 1426 Bx 1000	
"	5.V.17		2nd Lts. J.H HERBERT, H.E.C DICKIE, A.N GILMORE, & D.L CRIMP posted to Column	

Army Form C. 2118.

WAR DIARY
or
INTELLIGENCE SUMMARY of 30 D.A.C.
May 1917
(Erase heading not required.)

Place	Date	Hour	Summary of Events and Information	Remarks and references to Appendices
BOISLEUX AU-MONT	1/V/17		The guns of 148 Bde. were moved forward about 700 yards and 24 OF Wagons of No 1. Division were draws in consequence to make in moving forward the ammunition for these guns.	
"	2/V/17		Ammunition issued to Batteries 54 A. 544 AX 450 BX. Reconnoitre HENIN-SUR-COJEUL to select site for new forward Ammunition Dump. — Position selected at point N.32.a Enlgd. Sheet 57.c. Orders received to carry on at Boisleux dump pending further instructions. Ammunition issued to Batteries A.488 AX 1122 BX 576.	
"	3/V/17		Ammunition at Boisleux dump exhausted & Sections had to proceed to NEUVILLE-VITASSE and BEAURAINS to fill. Ammunition issued to Batteries A 7200 AX 4592 BX 2810	
"	4/V/17		No Ammunition on dump or in Echelon. Arrangement made with 78th Division and under their Orders Batteries draw Ammunition from 18 Spare Dumps to Complete Dumps at Guns up to 500 rounds per Gun and full Echelons. Ammunition drawn from 18 DAC A 3380 AX 1436 BX 1000.	
"	5/V/17		2 Lts. J.H. HERBERT H.E.C. DICKIE, A.N. GILMORE & D.L. CRIMP posted to Column	

WAR DIARY
or
INTELLIGENCE SUMMARY.   30. A.A.C.

(Erase heading not required.)

Army Form C. 2118.

Place	Date	Hour	Summary of Events and Information	Remarks and references to Appendices
BOISLEUX- AU-MONT	5.V.17		Instructions given on termination of Artillery Course at 3rd Army School	
	10.V.17		Lt. R.E. BURGESS, 2nd Lts. I.A.C. SAMSON, R.H. PEARSON, A.H. HUMPHREYS joined from Base & posted to Sections.	
	11.V.17		2nd Lt. N.L.L. Palmer posted to 13/149 Bde R.F.A. H.q of No 2. Section moved to point S.10.d.9.9. All Echelons complete to Establishment with Ammunition.	
"	19.V.17		Lt. W. Gray and Party of 26. O.R. proceed) to ABBEVILLE to get 50. Remounts	
Line of march	23.V.17		The Column withdrawn from the line and marches to HABARCQ Area today	
	24.V.17		marches to FOUFFLIN. RICAMETZ where A Echelon & B.q halted for the night	
			B. Echelon halted at TERNAS.	
"	25.V.17		H.q & A Echelon marches to AMETTES. B. Echelon to BELLERY	
"	26.V.17		H.q & No 1 Section march to BOESEGHEM - No. 2 Section to COHEM and B Echelon to THIENNES	
"	27.V.17		Column rests for the day	
"	28.V.17		Column marches to CAESTRE. Area billets at BORRE	
"	29.V.17		marches to HATOU	

WAR DIARY
or
INTELLIGENCE SUMMARY.

Army Form C. 2118.

30 A A E

Place	Date	Hour	Summary of Events and Information	Remarks and references to Appendices
BOISLEUX-AU-MONT	8.v.17		Instruction from our Nomination of Artillery Course at 3rd Army School.	
	10.v.17		Lt. R.E. BURGESS 2nd Lts. I.A.C. SAMSON, R.H. PEARSON, A.H. HUMPHREYS joined from Base.	
			Moved to Sultana.	
			2nd Lt. N.L.L. Palmer joined to B/149 Bde. RFA.	
			H.Q. & No.2 Section moved to point S.10.d.9.9.	
	11.v.17		H.Q. Echelon established. Establishment with Ammunition.	
	19.v.17		Lt. Halsey and party of 20. OR proceeded to ABBEVILLE to get 50 Remounts.	
Line of march	22.v.17		The Column withdrawn from the line and marched to HABARCQ Area. Every marked to FOUFFLIN RICOMETZ where A Echelon slept halted for the night.	
	24.v.17		B. Echelon halted at TERNAS.	
	25.v.17		H.Q. & A Echelon marches to AMETTES. B. Echelon to BELLERY	
	26.v.17		H.Q. & No.1 Section march to BOESEGHEM. No.2 Section to COHEM and B Echelon to THIENNES	
	27.v.17		Column rests for the day	
	28.v.17		Column marches to CAESTRE. Area billets at BORRE.	
	29.v.17		marches to WATOU.	

WAR DIARY
or
INTELLIGENCE SUMMARY.
(Erase heading not required.)

Army Form C. 2118.

30 APC
for May

Place	Date	Hour	Summary of Events and Information	Remarks and references to Appendices
Line of March	30.v.17		Rests at Hattu today.	
	31.v.17		Moved into Action at Point G.16.d.8.8. Ammunition dump established under Lt J Donnelly at G.16.d.97 Sheet 28. Ammunition taken over from X" Corps.	
			A. 11541. AX 5560 BX 6900	
	"		Trench mortar Ammunition 840 rds 9.45 inch, 4200 rds 2 inch, 14000 rds 3" Stokes	
			2328 N⁰ 5 Grenades	
			1920 23 ○	
			1404 V.P-A. 1"	
			308 V.P.A 1½"	
G.16.d.8.8	31.v.17		2nd Lt J.W. HERBERT posted to B/114g Bde in exchange with 2nd Lt J.H. KNIGHT	
	"		Flemish Interpreter MERTENS. joined for duty today.	
	"		Lt. Colonel John G.F. STANLEY CMG assuming duties of CRA during temporary absence of Brigadier General G.H.A. WHITE DSO. on leave.	
			C.J. Turner Lt Col. RFA
for O.C. 30 APC

17 June 1917

RFA
for O.C. 30 APC |

Army Form C. 2118.

3 DAC
for May

WAR DIARY
or
INTELLIGENCE SUMMARY.
(Erase heading not required.)

Instructions regarding War Diaries and Intelligence Summaries are contained in F. S. Regs., Part II. and the Staff Manual respectively. Title pages will be prepared in manuscript.

Place	Date	Hour	Summary of Events and Information	Remarks and references to Appendices
Line of March 30.v.17	30.v.17		Rests at Watou today.	
	31.v.17		Moves into Action at Point G.16.d.8.8. Ammunition dump established under Lt J Donnelly at G.16.a.97 Sheet 28. Ammunition taken over from X" Corps. A. 11501. B.A. 5560 B. 6900 Small Arms Ammunition 840 rds 9.45 inch, 4200 rds 2"inch 14000 rds 3" Stokes. 2325 No 5 Grenades 1920 — 23 " 1404 V.B.A. 1" 308 V.B.A. 1½"	
G.16.d.8.8.31.v.17			2nd Lt Oswd HERBERT posted to 31/149 Bde in exchange with 2nd Lt H KNIGHT (returned). Lt Herbert MERTENS joined for duty today. Lt Colonel John G.F. STANLEY C.M.G. assuming duties of C.R.A. during temporary absence of Brigadier General G.H.A WHITE. D.S.O. on leave.	

C Sturm
Lt RFA
for O.C. 30 DAC

1st June 1917

WAR DIARY or INTELLIGENCE SUMMARY

Army Form C. 2118.

30. T.M.C.
fr. June. 1917
Vol 19

Place	Date	Hour	Summary of Events and Information	Remarks and references to Appendices
G.16.d.&8	1.VI.17		A raft 31. O.R. reinforcements joined from Base. Lt. H. Brunwell sent to (Capt. Rawlins) for duty. Commenced dumping at Gun 900 rds for 18 pr. from of 750 rds for howitzers. A & C/148 Bdes on horseback taken to get their ammunition to the gun positions.	
	3.VI.17 to 4.VI.17		Heavy hostile shelling of L/148 Bde Gun positions with Lachrymatory gas shells during the getting of ammunition - known numbers at Gun position. Wagons safely brought away following night - 3 wounded killed 4-10 - an amazing unit 2 horses. 3 horses gassed slightly. 2 officers & 20 men (gunners) to Rest Camps at BOULOGNE for rest.	
	5.VI.17		Lt. Hagans detailed to army T.M. Equipment to the line - ammunition hostile shelling at ZILLEBEKE - one wagon struck by shell direct (heavy) - 2 mules wounded - no other casualties.	
	7.VI.17		much difficulty experienced in getting ammunition to Gun position of 148 Bde owing to heavy hostile shelling of road - 1 Animal killed.	
	VIII.VI.17		670 rounds T.M. ammunition delivered rds. to Lieutenant T.M. Batteries positions	

WAR DIARY or INTELLIGENCE SUMMARY

Army Form C. 2118.

30th TMC
June 1917.

Place	Date	Hour	Summary of Events and Information	Remarks and references to Appendices
G.16.d.8.8.	X.V.17		23 O.R. (total) to 748 Bn. 14 O.R. to 749 Bn. an reinforcements. Ammunition dump at H.13. Central taken over from 47th Divn.	
"	13.V.17		Guns moved from G.16.d.8.8. Sheet 28 as follows: No.1 Section to point G.30.a.3.3. HQ to 2 Sections to G.29.d.9.8.	
"	15.V.17		Reconnaissance (officers) new site for Ammunition dumps at H.27.C.	
G.29.d.9.8			Dumps at G.16.d.8.8. handed over to 8th Division.	
	16.V.17		Motor Cart used for conveying Rations to Howitzers T.M. Batteries on return destroyed during hostile shelling between TRANSPORT FARM and ZILLEBEKE.	
	17.V.17		Ammunition dumb at G.29.C. taken over from 41st Division. Experiment of getting Ammunition to Guns by means of Light Railway tried. 400 rds 18pr q 239 rds 4.5 How. Ammunition were taken up to G.30 Hostes I.13.a in G.S. Wagons and trails) on to trucks which were drawn by 10 mules (tractor) with long traces slaughterers. The Ammunition could only be got as far as point I.15.d.3.4. where the Ammunition was dumped. Scheme abandoned owing to approach of daylight. The amount of time taken in loading, unloading from G.S. Wagons to trucks, length, with the fact that the Railway track was unsuitable for Armed tractors, made the Scheme impracticable.	

Army Form C. 2118.

WAR DIARY
or
INTELLIGENCE SUMMARY.
(Erase heading not required.)

30 D.A.C.
June 1917

Place	Date	Hour	Summary of Events and Information	Remarks and references to Appendices
G.29.d.9.8.	18.6.17		Preparation of Site for dump at H.27.C.5.8 commenced.	
	21.6.17		Convoy 6. S.A. Wagons engaged in handing timber from KRUISTRAAT to ZILLEBEKE Shelled. 2 Wagons destroyed & 4 Animals wounded.	
	27.6.17		Dump at 24.73 central handed over to 8th Division and Ammunition Supply at G.24.d taken over from B. Corps Ammn Park	
	29.6.17		No. L/17530 Sergeant S.A. GRAHAM. B. Echelon awarded the Distinguished Conduct Medal for Gallantry in Action. Convoy of 11 S.A. Wagons returning from I.22.b. after delivering R.E. Material was heavily Shelled – one wagon totally destroyed, 1 mule killed and 3 wounded.	

30.6.17.

J.Gunn
Lt. R.D.
for O.C. 30 D.A.C.

Army Form C. 2118.

WAR DIARY
or
INTELLIGENCE SUMMARY.
(Erase heading not required.)

30th D.A.C.

fr. July 1917

WL 20

Place	Date	Hour	Summary of Events and Information	Remarks and references to Appendices
OUDERDOM	1.7.17		25D & 72D S.A.A. K & RN transp/lorries delivered to M.G. Offrs at HELLFIRE CORNER 72. Remounts arrived - Camps, Stables - no casualties. Major S. VICKERS and 2/Lt. J.T. BASENDALE, G.S. MAXWELL RN HILL and W.H. BORDASS joined from Base.	
	2.7.17		Convoy of 10 Lt. Haggs engaged in drawing timber heavily shelled at ZILLEBEKE 1 man (Driver J.E. Barker) killed and 1 horse killed and 3 wounded.	
	4.7.17		Reinforcements (48 O.R.) joined from Base.	
	8.7.17		Convoy 2 lorries with ammunition for 2/148 Bde shelled on approaching firing position Lt. Farrell wounded. 2 horses killed + 4 wounded. In spite of no horses & 1 lorry disabled great coolness + gallantry in steadying teams & drivers avoided stampeding the wounded horses during the hostile shelling	
	11.7.17		Fire occurred at ammunition dump at G dr. d. caused by spark from engine of a passing train. R.Sm. Smith and 2 A.B. Shortyoke displayed coolness and bravery by starting into the burning camouflage & removed towards the fire spreading along the dump. - no serious damage was done. Convoy of B Echelon convoying R.E. material to ZILLEBEKE shelled at H.H. MOIR Kus	

WAR DIARY of INTELLIGENCE SUMMARY

Army Form C. 2118.

30th Stge
1st July 1917

Place	Date	Hour	Summary of Events and Information	Remarks and references to Appendices
OUDERDOM	1.7.17		250 rnds S.A.A. K.I.A. handed to Lt. M.G. Officer HELLFIRE CORNER. 72 Remounts arrived - (Canada Stores) - no casualties. Major S. Vickers and 2/Lt. J.T. Basendale. G.S. Maxwell, R.N. Hill and W.H. Bordass joined from Base.	
	2.7.17		Convoy of 10 G.S. Wagons engaged in drawing timber heavily shelled at ZILLEBEKE. 1 man (Driver J.E. Bates) killed and 1 horse killed and 3 wounded.	
	4.7.17		Reinforcements (48 O.R.) joined from Base.	
	8.7.17		Convoy 6 Wagons with ammunition to 148 Bde. Shelled in approaching gun position. Lt. Farwell wounded. 2 horses killed, 4 wounded. In spite of his wounds Lt. Farwell displayed great courage & gallantry in steadying horses & Drivers, & extricating the wounded horses during the hostile shelling.	
	11.7.17		Fire occurred at ammunition dump at G.H.Q. 2nd d. Caused by spark from Engine of a passing train. R.S.M. Goot Sergt. Saye & 3/men who drafted up Contour and Convoys by checking into the morning Ammunition Wagons towards the fire spreading along the dump. - no serious damage was done. Convoy of B. Echelon Conveying R.E. timber to ZILLEBEKE shelled. Dr. H. Moir killed.	

WAR DIARY
or
INTELLIGENCE SUMMARY.

Army Form C. 2118.

30 Apr

Place	Date	Hour	Summary of Events and Information	Remarks and references to Appendices
OUDERDOM			and 1 Mule wounded) — Convoy of 4 Wagons from No 1 Section conveying Ammunition to Gun Position (Shells) — Spr R. Jones, A.B. Sutton & H.W. Spooner & 4 mules wounded — 4 Mules Killed	
"	12.7.17		Convoy of 4 Wagons from No 2 Section conveying Ammunition to Guns (Shells) S.S. Christie N.C. & Lt Harrison & L./Cpl. McCarthy L. wounded — 4 horses Killed and 10 Wounded.	
"			Convoy of "B" Echelon Conveying T.M. Bombs to 2nd Mortar Battery (Shells) Dr H Beasley Killed & Cpl H Gratton wounded.	
"	13.7.17		Convoy of "B" Echelon with Trench Mortar Bombs (Shells) at 2H.06.d.8.3. Dr E. Rose wounded (and also 2 mules wounded)	
"	16.7.17		Convoy of No 1 Section with Ammunition for the Gun Positions lost up during attack by enemy Aeroplanes. S.E. Pethersen, Decr. Lee-murder) (Horses Killed — Dr J.J. Pymond an) Q Stokes wounded. 1 horse Killed & 2 horses wounded) 3. 2 horses wounded (by Shrap)	
"	17.7.17		Pte S. Doug, Dr v. Grant wounded (no. Self wounding) (military med). W.C. Hurley, Mr L./Sgt. A.W. Furnell (wounded) (military med.) Mr Suerich	
"	17.18.19		A Echelon lived on La Cruble to Smithlane at 14.5. Bde as a thing den 45. & 29 July.	
			7 w Bombs for Guns for Poelcheu. Bde W. have taken over three sectors.	

WAR DIARY or INTELLIGENCE SUMMARY

Army Form C. 2118

Place	Date	Hour	Summary of Events and Information	Remarks and references to Appendices
OUDERDOM			and 1 Mule wounded. — Convoy of Wagons from No. 1 Section conveying Ammunition to Gun position Shelled — Gnr R. Jones, A.B. Sutton & H. Foreman & 6 mules wounded. - 4 mules killed.	
"	10.7.17		Convoy of Wagons from No 2 Section conveying Ammunition to Guns Shelled. S.S. Chruche H/ Lt Hanson H. & Lt McCarthy L wounded. — 4 horses killed and 10 Horses Convoy of B Echelon Conveying T.M. Bomb to Trench mortar Batteries Shelled. Dr. H. Bentley killed & Corpl. N. Cadilla wounded	
"	13.7.17		Convoy of B. Echelon with Trench mortar Bombs Shelled at ZILLEBEKE. Dr. H. Rose wounded and other 2 mules wounded	
"	16.7.17		Convoy of No 1 Section with ammunition for the Gun Battery which are being taken by the Australians of 9 Bdes. encountered Hostile Shelling. Dr J. S. Rumney and g. Slade wounded 1 horse killed 2 horses & 3 Horses L.12 horses Slightly Scored Men 71049 Dr Norwood wounded but still on duty	
"	16.7.17		No L/5290. Dr A H Farnell awarded military medal for gallantry	
"	17,18,19 & 20 July		& B Echelon turned on to replace old Gun positions of 148 Bde of 47 Aug Bde to 700 rounds per Gun. for Australian Bdes. who have taken over these positions.	

Army Form C. 2118

WAR DIARY
or
INTELLIGENCE SUMMARY
(Erase heading not required.)

To A.D.C.
Fr. [?] Sept 1917

Place	Date	Hour	Summary of Events and Information	Remarks and references to Appendices
OUDERDOM	27/7/17		B.s.w. took baths from Base to "B" Echelon to billets in rest [?]	
	28/7/17		9 Waggon B.F. Echelon Carried S.A.A. No 5, 28 Ross Street Stoke Bank K.P.S. afor from [?] Bomb Store to BELGIAN CORNER I.22.b.5.7	
			Six 25 Waggons to Sutton became [?] for Brigade bombardment - 11 [?]	
	29/7/17		Bombardment	
	30/7/17		[?] started on travels with [?] under Copl. marched to Brown [?] the Infantry Section of Advanced Park Train, recorded 80 gy at [?] Advanced Bomb Store for [?] to Army Bombardment and 85 [?] 2 Mobile dumps which are being established in "D" and [?] A/W921 [?] A RITCHIE No 1 Sutton "B" gone down to attend at response 7.3 E Bomber held Camoufleter Convoys Engine Section of 11M Pontoon through Battery at I 21.6.6.05.	
	31/7/17		In the attack today No. H9007 Driver E.P. Phillipson and No. 3182 Dr. Cluck "B" Echelon were wounded.	
			Lt. H. T. E. Baltman [?] wounds to [?]	

C.Burns Lt. RM
D.S.E. OC 3rd sec RM

31.7.17

Army Form C. 2118

WAR DIARY
or
INTELLIGENCE SUMMARY
(Erase heading not required.)

To ... A.P.C.
from July 1917

Place	Date	Hour	Summary of Events and Information	Remarks and references to Appendices
OUDERDOM	27.7.17		B.S.M. Hush took from Base to B Echelon to establish ammy ore dush firmamp	
	28.7.17		9 Wagons B. & Echelon Covered SAA 105.33 in from So Stokes Bomb 1200 flares from Command Arms Store to SHELTER CORNER I 22 b.6.7	
	29.7.17		Sgt QC Hooper M.1. Section proceed to gun positions with ammunition - 1 man wounded - Browne Rose	
	30.7.17		H2 Drivers 43 Animals took Packsaddles and 2n Capt. travelled & Gunners forming the Infantry Section of Armoured Pack Showe Reserves Friday at the Command Bomb Store for Mountain Trench Ammunition and RE material. 6 Mules Drivers killed, 41 men wounded on 2nd day L.4.54481 Bomb H RITCHIE No. 1. Section 2 stops [?] in action at POPERINGHE 768 wounded. Lahti Ammunition Convoys & firm positions of 1st Australian troops Battery at I 21 6.6.05.	
	31.7.17		In the attack Early 96 140007 Gunner F P Phillipson and M 3182 Dr. C. Luke 13th Echelon was wounded. In the T E Balhman grows wounded in Pontoon.	

31.7.17

C. Shurson L. RM
OC 3. ABC RFA

War Diary Vol. 21
==
36th Bde. R.F.A.
month of August 1917

Army Form C. 2118.

30th D.A.C.

WAR DIARY or INTELLIGENCE SUMMARY.

(Erase heading not required.)

for August 1917

Place	Date	Hour	Summary of Events and Information	Remarks and references to Appendices
OUDERDOM	1.8.17 to 4.8.17		Continual downpours of Rain - Attacks to the gun positions impossible for wagons owing to mud. Small difficulty experienced in getting ammunition forward.	
	5.8.17		Came under orders of 18th Div. Arty H.Q. today. Dumps at Guns to be increased to 800 rounds per 18pr, and 600 rnds per 4.5" How. These amounts must be up at guns by 8th instant. Subsequent orders received to the effect that in view of traffic regulations it has been found impossible to get the ongoing amounts of ammunition to guns - therefore dumps will be maintained at 600 and 400 respectively. Wagon Lines Shells by horses H.V. Gun - no Casualties. 1 18pr. S.F. wagon damaged to No 2 Section damaged.	
"	7.8.17			
"	11.8.17		30 Divisional Artillery withdrawn from the line & proceeds to STEENWERCK Area - A & B échelons & H.Q. marches to Camp at G.9.c.5.2 Sheet 36.A. B. Échelon marches to Camp at L.17.6.2.9.	
G.9.c.5.2 Sheet 36 a	15.8.17		Column marches to STRAZEELE Area and (arrived at ROUGE CROIX Reinforcements 76 L.D horses & 33 mules arrived from CALAIS today.	
ROUGE CROIX				

Army Form C. 2118

WAR DIARY
or
INTELLIGENCE SUMMARY 30th D.A.C. for August 1917

(Erase heading not required.)

Instructions regarding War Diaries and Intelligence Summaries are contained in F.S. Regs., Part II. and the Staff Manual respectively. Title Pages will be prepared in manuscript.

Place	Date	Hour	Summary of Events and Information	Remarks and references to Appendices
DRANOUTRE.	24/8/17		Column Marched to DRANOUTRE AREA.	
	31/8/17		33 L.D. Mds review from BOULOGNE.	

W.O.E. [signature]
Lt. Col. [illegible] 30 DAC

Army Form C. 2118.

WAR DIARY
or
INTELLIGENCE SUMMARY.   30th D.A.C.   for SEPTEMBER 1917
(Erase heading not required.)

Vol 2 2

Place	Date	Hour	Summary of Events and Information	Remarks and references to Appendices
DRANOUTRE.	Sept 1st		DVI A.R.P. taken over from 4th Australian D.A.C. (T.I.C.Z.S.) S.O. a T.M. Amn. Dump at DE KENNEBAK. Work carried on at LA POLKA with a view to the concentration of large quantities of Ammunition to the expense closing down of the A.R.P. at LINDENHOEK.	
	Sept 4		DVI A.R.P. & the DE KENNEBAK Dump handed over to 14th Division. Nights of Sept 3/4 4/5 Ammunition sent up from Rietpoort dist to Gun Positions via La POLKA. Delivered to Guns 9600 A, 16000 AX, 3600 BX. Remainder of LA POLKA 4800 A, 4000 AX, 4500 BX. DAC Echelon supplied to Batteries & ↑direct from LINDENHOEK.	
	Sept 8		A working party of 400 men from 49th DA at VIERSTRAAT & G.S. Wagons supplied by 30th D.A.C. to be attached to work in forty. The party taken on motor lorries of De Selores from 10 & Sept.	

Army Form C. 2118

WAR DIARY
or
INTELLIGENCE SUMMARY 38th D.A.C. for September 1917
(Erase heading not required.)

Instructions regarding War Diaries and Intelligence Summaries are contained in F. S. Regs., Part II. and the Staff Manual respectively. Title Pages will be prepared in manuscript.

Place	Date	Hour	Summary of Events and Information	Remarks and references to Appendices
DRANOUTRE Section	Sept 13 to Sept 28		Daily convoys delivering Ammunition to Guns owing to a train getting off the rails at LA POLKA. A breakdown gang of Gunners assisted in the horse ozone.	
	Sept 29		Gunners assisted in carrying Ammunition to Guns & men brought up. Fatigue work. West working for the 250 Gunnery L. of C. I 33 a.d.S. 3 o.r. wounded by shell fire. Bomb dropped by hostile Aircraft near No. 1 Section line. No casualties.	
	Sept 30		Bomb dropped on fr POLKA DUMP. 1 member to O.R. wounded.	

Officer by i/c Record R.72
Col 30 D.A.C.

WAR DIARY or INTELLIGENCE SUMMARY

Army Form C. 2118.

20 —7—
1st October 1917 Vol 2

Place	Date	Hour	Summary of Events and Information	Remarks and references to Appendices
DRANOUTRE	1.10.17		N° 43493 Driver H. LATHAN, N° 2 Section and 880708 Driver H. LEESE, B. Echelon died of wounds and buried at OUTTERSTEENE today. Return sheets to Salve Ammunition from positions received by 49th Div. Hdy. N°2 Section cleared 3079 B.X. from positions issued by D/246 at O.14.a.7.3 (Sheet 28 – 40000) N°3 Section cleared 1560 A, 500 A.X., 73 A Smoke from position O.13.c.8.8 (Sheet 28 – 40000) issued by A/124 at 0.13.c.8.8 (Sheet 28 – 40000) N°1 Section attempted to salve the ammunition at A/245 position 0.9.c.6.6 (Sheet 28 40000). It was found impossible to get waggons to the position owing to the state of the ground & hostile shell fire. Lorries 1 mule killed 4 mules wounded. 1 horse wounded. See the above Salvage ammunition delivered at LA POLKA by the Hdy. and Party of 45 men found by the Column to empty an empty Battery & Waggon Lines & Headquarters at N32 l.11 + N33 c.64	
	3/10			

Army Form C. 2118.

WAR DIARY or INTELLIGENCE SUMMARY.

30th D.A.C. for October 1917

(Erase heading not required.)

Place	Date	Hour	Summary of Events and Information	Remarks and references to Appendices
DRANOUTRE	3/10		Empty Box, Cartridge boxes + 18 pdr Ammn. taken from O.27.a.	
	5/10		1 Charge, 1 Rider + 20 LD Mules arrived. Charge + Rider posted to Bowman. The 20 Mules to the Columns.	
			10 B.S. Wagons sent to Div. Bomb Store at N.29.c.5.6. to Div'ne Bomb Sta. to New Store at N.21.d.7.3.	
	12/10		237 Pr. A. 263 M. AX Salved from hostile bny. at 0.13.a.55.10 returned to LA POLKA	
	13/10		Ptes. S + J. Walker joined from 29th Div. Posted to 161 Section	
	17/10		Mess Relion Sergeant Corp Connors (Col. Sgn.) to these Wilson sick duty	
			Coffin + Rev 30th Div. Reserve Connelle Rev. No. N32.c.5.5. A party of 50 tons proceeded from the Column to the Bowsing boundle dem Reller.	

Lt. J. R. Wilson M.C. R.S.M. O.F. Frost (Mention Mate) Bt. T.J. Foodsen (Mentere Mate) B.Q.M.S. J. Morrison (D.C.M.) Sgt. S.A. Graham (D.C.M.) Dr. A.H. Farrell (Mentry Mate)

Army Form C. 2118

WAR DIARY
or
INTELLIGENCE SUMMARY

(Erase heading not required.) 30th D.A.C. for Coleta (9¹)

Place	Date	Hour	Summary of Events and Information	Remarks and references to Appendices
DRANOUTRE	18/7		No. 82279 Gn. A. McManus (No. 2 Section) died of wounds on 15/7/02 No. 18 (Chicago U.S.A.) Ypres Hospital.	
	22/7		Nose keyed shutter.	
	28/7		32 + D Horr now out for Barrage. Throughout the week the platoon was employed largely on fatigues & continued work of ammunition in sheds. for forward area — Issue began :— A5977, AX 5052, BX 4729. A Smoke 73.	

Arthur Capper?
N/ for O.C. 30 DM.

2.11.17

Army Form C. 2118.

WAR DIARY
or
INTELLIGENCE SUMMARY. 30 Sqd RE
(Erase heading not required.)

November 1917   Vol 2

Place	Date	Hour	Summary of Events and Information	Remarks and references to Appendices
DRANOUTRE	1.11.17		Ammunition Salved by No 2 Section + returned to ZA DUMP. A Smoke 294. B Smoke 515 BCBR 140 (from O.3.b.3.8. O.3.c.3.5)	
	4.11.17		Handing Over Scheme (of Hottent in Lorgeon + suggested improvements of Balk Standing etc.) drawn up + submitted to Headquarters.	
	5.11.17		500 A Smoke drawn from T.1.C.2.4. (Dv1) + delivered to ZA DUMP. 392 A Smoke drawn from C/149 (O.B.C.30.0b) + delivered to 3/10th (13rd at O.B.b.4.1.) C/10th (25F at O.B. C.15-36)	
	9.11.17		213.4. 33 Br unserviceable cylinders from O.X.a.5.2. (A/148) L+ A unserviceable from O.19.d.42 (13/148) + handed over to Salvage (a)	
	19.11.17		LA POLKA A.R.P. handed over to 3rd Australian Division and HALLEBAST and BORDENBURG ARP's taken over by Column from 39 division - N.2.d. sheet 28	
	21.11.17		The Column relieved by 5rd Australian ARP + marched to ZEVECOTEN. HQ. + cars at G.35.c.4.6. A Echelon Ordnance Camp. M4.c.9.6. B Echelon G.35.d.1.5. Sheet 28.	
ZEVECOTEN	27.11.17		The Re-organisation of the Column vide M.2. August No & 2. Carried out with effect from today under instruction from S.A.O. No. 13/245 dt. 14.11.17 (3s division Mystats dt 7.11.17)	
	29.11.17		Lt H.P. FITZGERALD proceeds to England to take up duties. O Jung Capt RE 30 Div RE 1.12.17

T2134. Wt. W708—776. 500000. 4/15. Sir J. C. & S.

Army Form C. 2118.

30 D.A.C
for Dec 1917

WM 25

WAR DIARY
or
INTELLIGENCE SUMMARY.
(Erase heading not required.)

Place	Date	Hour	Summary of Events and Information	Remarks and references to Appendices
ZEVECOTEN	1.12.17		No 1 & 2 Sections engaged in destroying 250 rounds the 18pr gun at the position - Could not destroy	
	2.12.17		A further 200 rounds for gun to be dumped at gun position of 38/143 & C.149. No 1 & 2 Sections engaged under the	
	3.12.17		17 S.A. Haggais & 73 Brig. Whalers sent to assist 2nd Infantry Bde to throw	
			Lt. Col. Hon. G.F. Stanley Ch. of S. acting CRA during absence on leave of Brigadier General Stapylton D.S.O.	
	5.12.17		1. Team from No. 1 Section Sabres & Troops 4.5" Howitzers at I.17.d.6.6. Allyps Battery to Feb 6.39. a.s.a.	
			& sent to No 18 Light O mobile workshop	
			2. Howitzer 4.5 inch Sabres by No 2 Section from various batteries at I.17.d.6.6. Allyps Battery to 39 a.s.a.	
	7.12.17		1. Team from No 1 Section (Salvo) a troop to Ypres at I.17.A.6.1	
	9.12.17		18 Surplus S.A. H. a gun hands (N.4. Ordnance No Corps group	
			Surplus harness consigned on distribution sent to Base Ordnance store	
	13.12.17		One strong wash heavy & party from No. 1 Section reinforcement to June 2 18pr guns from a	
	16.12.17		varied position at I.23.a.6.5. Allyps to have been left by an Australian Bde in July. Succeeded in	
			getting the guns out of their position with great difficulty but owing to the ground being very much shaken	
			up by shell fire taken the 5th batt. have wanted by hostile shelling the guns were only got away	
			about 1 mile further from the position when they became bogged in very soft ground - 2 horses kills being	
	18.12.17		1. Team from No 1 Section after great difficulty salved one 18pr gun (Trype) at I.23.a.6.5.	

WAR DIARY or INTELLIGENCE SUMMARY

Army Form C. 2118.

2nd Sheet

30 [Squadron] MGC
[1st Dec 1917]

(Erase heading not required.)

Instructions regarding War Diaries and Intelligence Summaries are contained in F.S. Regs., Part II. and the Staff Manual respectively. Title pages will be prepared in manuscript.

Place	Date	Hour	Summary of Events and Information	Remarks and references to Appendices
ZEYECOTEN	19.12.17		Owing to very hard frost much difficulty experienced in getting ammunition to guns.	
	20.12.17		One 18 pr gun of one 18 pr Carriage kept Buffs between fixed SOS by No 1 Section from I.24.a.8.9. & I.18.c.33 positions & taken to Ordnance while Horstairp made difficulty experienced in getting ammunition to 18 pr gun positions — many numerous shell holes and forge nature of ground. Haynes slipped into shell holes about 2 sm yards from position — 3 mounted with Jocks sent into like. Ammunition packed from the rigged. Haynes to position — horses shell-dropping harnessed. Both positions — no Casualties among men — but one horse was killed.	
	21.12.17		One 18 pr Gun of Carriage with broken Axle SOS by No 2 Section from I.24.a position sent to Ordnance. One 4.5" Carriage of 18 pr Carriage — took [relief] SOS from I.23.a.3.6 and two 18 pr howitzer Howitzer SOS from I.18.C.3.3 by No 1 Section. Sent to Hackerlyn (No 18 sqdn). Captain C.F. TURNER, Lieutenant J.G. DONNELLY, Sergeant H.B. WHITE, Corporal T. HUDSON and Army H. SMITHAM mentioned in Commander in Chief's Despatch for distinguished service & Devotion to duty — London Gazette dated 11th December 1917.	
	22.12.17		1. 18 pr Gun & Carriage SOS by No 1 Section from I.23.b.00.45.	
	23.12.17		1. 18 pr Gun damaged took buffer of Carriage two wheels & trail SOS by No 1 Section from I.22.b.2.6.	
	[24.12.17]		& latter 18 pr Carriage SOS from I.22.b.2.6. by No 1 Section.	

Army Form C. 2118.

3rd Sheet

WAR DIARY
or
INTELLIGENCE SUMMARY. 30 A.T.C. for December 1917

(Erase heading not required.)

Place	Date	Hour	Summary of Events and Information	Remarks and references to Appendices
ZEVECOTEN	27.12.17		Two 18th June Salvos by No 1. Section from I.18 c.8.1. enemies position.	
	28.12.17		1. 18pr Gun Salvo by No 2. Section from I.22.c.2.6. enemies position	
	30.12.17		1. 18pr Gun Salvo by No 1. Section from I.23.b.0.4	

G.F. Headingwell Rowe O.C.
O/C. 30 D.A.C.

Army Form C. 2118.

WAR DIARY or INTELLIGENCE SUMMARY.

(Erase heading not required.)

of J 30. Bgc

for Jany 1918

VII 26

Place	Date	Hour	Summary of Events and Information	Remarks and references to Appendices
ZEVECOTEN	31.1.18		1 or 4.5 Howitzer & 1 Howitzer Carriage with no fuses salved from I.24.b.7.6. and I.22.b.6.1. Positions by No. 142 Section - all in a battered condition. Handed over to Ordnance Railhead OUDERDOM. Since 22nd Nov. 1917 13, 18 pr. Guns and 11, 4.5 Howitzer with Carriages & several Carriages with no "breech" blocks were salved by the Column under considerable difficulties & taken over nearly all by many hostile fire. - G.O.C. R.A. IX Corps sent a congratulatory letter on the Work performed by 2nd & 3rd Sections this part.	
GODEWAERSVELDE	4.1.18		Column relieved by 37th Division & marched to GODEWAERSVELDE Area (XI 24 X 3) via RENINGHELST - WESTOUTRE - BERTHEN - SCHAEXKEN - X 4. C. During the journey the Tractors were divided by the 50th Division at WESTOUTRE.	
MORBECQUE	5.1.18		Column marched to MORBECQUE Area via FLETRE - STRAZEELE - PRADELLES - BORRE - HAZEBROUCK	
RENESCURE	6.1.18		Column marched to RENESCURE via WALLON - CAPPEL - EBBLINGHEM to Hutts in T. 19. 20 & 25 the 1st Section	
	8.1.18		Headquarters marched to STEENBECQUE and entrained for BOVES Area. - detrained at LONGUEAU & marched to BERTEAUCOURT. - Weather intensely cold & frozen state of roads made marching very difficult	
	9.1.18		No 2 Section marched to STEENBECQUE and entrained for BOVES Area - detrained at LONGUEAU & marched to BERTEAUCOURT.	
	10.1.18		No 3 Section marched and entrained at STEENBECQUE for BOVES Area detrained at LONGUEAU & marched to BERTEAUCOURT.	

T2134. Wt. W708-776. 500000. 4/15. Sir J. C. & S.

Army Form C. 2118.

Sheet 2

WAR DIARY
or
INTELLIGENCE SUMMARY.
(Erase heading not required.)

30 Bty RFA
for Jany 18

Place	Date	Hour	Summary of Events and Information	Remarks and references to Appendices
BERTEAUCOURT	12.1.18		Column marched to HANGEST via MOREUIL - PLESSIER - ROZAINVILLERS	
HANGEST	13.1.18		Column marched to ROYE via AMIENS - ROYE Road and billets in the town	
ROYE	19.1.18		Column marched to ROUY-LE-PETIT. (H Qrs & No 1 Section) BUNY (No 2 Section) OFFOY (No 3 Section) via NESLE. and billeted in the respective villages named.	
OFFOY	20.1.18 to 31.1.18		In Rest Billets. - Units engaged in training as per programme of drills. Vehicles & equipment overhauled.	

2.2.18

C. Gunn Capt. RFA
Commdg. 30 Bty RFA

Army Form C. 2118.

WAR DIARY
or
INTELLIGENCE SUMMARY.
(Erase heading not required.)

Place	Date	Hour	Summary of Events and Information	Remarks and references to Appendices
OFFOY	9.2.18		Belgian CROIX-DE-GUERRE awarded to No 2793 Dr. J. Cosgrove and No 67523 Dr. H. Olivers for gallantry in action at YPRES.	
	11.2.18		Mounted & foot - drill orders - for inspection by CRA.	
	13.2.18		Mounted Parade - drill orders for inspection by Commander, 2nd Div. Artlly at ERCHEU.	
	20.2.18		Column moves into action & marches via VOYENNES - BUVY-NATOMY-TOULE-SANCOURT to billets VILLER ST-CHRISTOPHE.	
VILLERS St. CHRISTOPHE	28.2.18		Adomis Ammunition Dump (new) at JAMY and ROUPY. to take about 2793 No. 18 pr. & 10000 Relr. Br. 30 3 A.R.P. established at K.11.a 3.4. Sheet 66.Cl (Av 13.16 N.E.) 6.1 3F Magrs 18 pr. & 6 Magrs 4.5. I hr Ammunition taken to gun position of C/148. and D/148. respectively. 3. 6" T.M. Howitzer drawn from O.C. Corps Arty 14 DM and 220 rounds of 6" T.M. Ammunition taken up to T.M position.	

1.3.18

Army Form C. 2118.

WAR DIARY
or
INTELLIGENCE SUMMARY.
(Erase heading not required.)

1st Sheet

30 DAC
March 18

Vol 28

Place	Date	Hour	Summary of Events and Information	Remarks and references to Appendices
VILLERS ST CHRISTOPHE	1.3.18		18. Q.F Magna ÷6. 4.5 How Magns of Ammunition taken to gun positions of 148 Bde by No 1. Section.	
			18 Q.F Magns do. 4.5 How Magns of Ammunition taken to gun positions of 149 Bde by No 2 Section	
			Advanced ammunition dumps at SAVY & ROUPY established. Personnel removed to Hessian dugouts at AUBIGNY	
	3.3.18		1. 6" Howitzer guns drawn from no Cotn South Ham & delivered together with 40 Rds 6" Ammunition to T.M. Battery at ROUPY.	
	18.3.18		588 rounds 18X taken to gun positions of 149 3 Bdes by No 2 Sections and 150 Rds T.M Ammn	
			2" Ditto to L'EPINE DE DALLON Redoubt.	
	19.3.18		412 Rds 18X and 2" Rds 4.5 taken to Gun positions of C+D Batteries 149 Bdes and	
			150 Rds T.M Ammn taken to MANCHESTER Hill Redoubt.	
VILLERS ST CHRISTOPHE	21.3.18	4 am	Enemy attack commenced. Wagon lines shelled – one Casualties. Telephone Communication cut by hostile shelling. No 1 & 2. Sections keenly engaged in Supplying Ammunition. The few Grenade Wagons sent forward. Lieut Hon G.F Stanley admitted to Field Ambulance (35th) Sick – Cash C Subsection assumed Command. 2nd Lt Magno destroyed by shell fire at SAVY, 1 Driver killed and 2 wounded 2333 Pte J Large transport return order to withdraw at once to EPPEVILLE – Unanticipated from infantry for S.A.A & Grenade	
	22.3.18	2.Am	Met by Sgt Sutton	
EPPEVILLE	"	2 pm	Orders to withdraw to Gun ground S.E of ESMERY HALLON received. All Sections engaged in Supplying gun Ammn & S.A.A and Grenades.	

Army Form C. 2118.

WAR DIARY
or
INTELLIGENCE SUMMARY.
(Erase heading not required.)

Jor Shul
30 Lyn
Jor March 1918

Place	Date	Hour	Summary of Events and Information	Remarks and references to Appendices
ESMERY HALLON	23.3.18	6. P.m.	Moved to OGNOLLES - Ammunition dumps established at OGNOLLES and SOLENTE. Urgent attend for Ammunition from the 14th & Army Bde & 9th Bde. (30 Div.) met - Dump at OGNOLLES light weeks).	
OGNOLLES	24.3.18	8 p.m.	Moved to SOLENTE. S.A.A. Section had frequent appeals for Ammunition and grenades	
SOLENTE	"	4 p.m.	Moved to CHAMPIEN (thereby) on the front S.S.E. of CHAMPIEN - Ammunition dump formed at CHAMPIEN. Serious attack opened over 2,000,000 rounds S.A.A. issued.	
CHAMPIEN	25.3.18	8 p.m.	Moved to ROUY forward via ROIGLISE - ROYE Road	
ROIGLISE	"	11 a.m.	Moved to BEUVRAIGNES via ROYE - LAUCOURT - TILLOLOY under orders of 62nd French Division	
BEUVRAIGNES	26.3.18	4 a.m.	Moved to GRIVILLERS via TILLOLOY - POPIECOURT - Ammunition dump established at GRIVILLERS	
GRIVILLERS	"	10 a.m.	S.A.A. Section motors to join 30 Division infantry at ARVILLERS	
"	"	1 p.m.	Moved to FAVEROLLES	
FAVEROLLES	"	8 p.m.	Hqrs No.2 Section reformed & FONTAINE-SOUS-MONTDIDIER via MONTDIDIER. No.1 Section reformed on arrival)	
"	"	"	Section for Ammunition Supply.	
FONTAINE-SOUS-	27.3.18	11:30 a.m	No.1 Section reformed Column - Orders received to join 30th Division and move towards PLESSIER-ROZAINVILLERS	
MONTDIDIER			via MARESTMONTIERS - HARGICOURT. - On arrival at HARGICOURT orders were received to proceed to MAILLY-RAINEVAL via Central Subsection - 3 lorries of Ammunition received & Corbets Echelon	
MAILLY-RAINEVAL	28.3.18	3 p.m.	Moved to MERVILLE-au-Bois - under orders of 133rd French Division - S.A.A. Section forthwith under orders	

T2134. Wt. W708—776. 500000. 4/15. Sir J. C. & S.

Army Form C. 2118.

WAR DIARY
or
INTELLIGENCE SUMMARY. 3rd Div. T.
(Erase heading not required.)

3rd Sheet

for March 1918

Place	Date	Hour	Summary of Events and Information	Remarks and references to Appendices
			of 3rd Division beforward to JALEUX trestrian with orders outs of the Division for a point near ABBEVILLE for Re-organisation. Ammunition Dumps at ROUVREL	
MERVILLE-AU-BOIS	29.3.18	9 pm	moved to open ground on JUMEL-ORESMAUX Road near JUMEL - ROUVREL Ammunition during Ephemerals	
JUMEL	31.3.18	11 am	HQ No 1 & 2 Sections moved to BERNY-SUR-NOYE - Ammunition Dumps at ESTREES-GUYENCOURT Road and at farm near BOIS DESRAMEES on JUMEL-ORESMAUX.	

1st April 1918.

[signature]
Lieut. for O.C. 3rd Div. T.

T2134. Wt. W708—776. 500000. 4/15. Sir J. C. & S.

Army Form C. 2118.

WAR DIARY
or
INTELLIGENCE SUMMARY.
(Erase heading not required.)

3 Army C
1st April 1918

Vol 29

Place	Date	Hour	Summary of Events and Information	Remarks and references to Appendices
BERNY-SUR-NOYE	1.4.18		Bombarded ESSERTAUX - ROSSIGNOL and FLERS-SUR-NOYE for positions on its West of withdrawal from present position. - No 1 & 2 Sections engaged in blowing ammn to gun positions - S/s Hagon Napping Battery Sektion. 2nd Lt BOOTH 336 Bde RFA & M OR Stragglers from various divisions joined here from RAILWAY VERS. 7 O/s wounded. Lt "A" P.F.R Bde attached on Logon. W/ers Bde. - Remaining 14. OR allotted on roll. 4 2 Sections finding further instructions - 2nd Lt Booth sent from his Bde at GUYENCOURT. 2 motor Ambulances attached to no from 96 FA Medical came for evacuating Sick & Wounded	
BERNY-SUR-NOYE	3.4.18		The S/s Hagon of Column moved back together with Sick Animals to ROSSIGNOL - S/s Hagon only of No 1 & 2 Sections remaining at BERNY to maintain Ammunition Supply. - 2nd Lt JEVESON and Party of 19 OR from 30 M.T. Sent to North or Ammunition Dump established for 30 Divisional Artillery at BOIS DESRAMÉES, near the farm.	
	4.4.18		2nd Lt F Shepherd sent to POIX to conduct 7 S/s Hagon coming from ABBEVILLE to rejoin Column. 12 Pairs of Leaders with harness sent from No 1 Section to 748 Bde & 17 "bare" leaders from No 2 Section sent to 149 Bde to assist batteries to horse their Guns. - Column moved to ESSERTAUX at 3pm. 10. S/s Hagons sent under 2nd Lt Huits and parked at FREMONTIERS. to rejoin Column tomorrow. 14 "HFA Bde (7 teams) and 148 Bde (3 teams) owing to shortage of horses caused by casualties in Skill join tomorrow.	
ESSERTAUX	5.5.18		10 teams sent to horse Hagons parked at FREMONTIERS & horsey Some spare teams at TALEUX - return	

Army Form C. 2118.

Instructions regarding War Diaries and Intelligence Summaries are contained in F. S. Regs., Part II. and the Staff Manual respectively. Title pages will be prepared in manuscript.

3rd Sheet 30th DTR

WAR DIARY
or
INTELLIGENCE SUMMARY.
(Erase heading not required.)

for April 1918

Place	Date	Hour	Summary of Events and Information	Remarks and references to Appendices
ESSERTAUX	5.4.18		To return to ESSERTAUX from Longueau by lorries. The 7 S.A.H. gone sent on from PRIX ESSALEUX to await arrival of the Column.	
	7.4.18		Hdq Nos 1 & 2 Sections with 748 & 749 Batns moved to SALEUX.	
SALEUX	8.4.18		7. Siamese unit to 74" P.E. 13th RFA returned to Column as the Bn had been made up with horses.	
	9.4.18		Hdq DTR moved to FERM. PETIT QUESNEL about 2 kilometres S.H. of SALEUX station.	
FERM.PETIT QUESNEL	10.4.18		Lt. Stafford & Advance Party proceeded by lorry to POPERINGHE to arrange billets - DTR reporting to station master for entraining at St Roch. Station AMIENS at 19.47 (cancelled) - moved to BELLOY-SUR-SOMME	
	11.4.18		Arrangements for entraining at St Roch cancelled.	
BELLOY-SUR-SOMME	12.4.18	9 pm	Moved to CANDAS via FLIXECOURT - ST OUEN - CANAPLES - MONTRELET.	
CANDAS	13.4.18	6 pm	Moved to GEZAINCOURT via LONGUEVILLETTE.	
GEZAINCOURT	14.4.18	4 pm	Moved to DOULLENS and entrained at Midday for CASSEL. On arrival at HAZEBROUCK train shelled - no casualties - detrained at ARNEKE at 7 pm instead of CASSEL and marched to HONDEGHEM via ST MARIE CAPPEL to P. 31. Sheet 27	
P. 31.	16.4.18	2 pm	Moved to L. 35.d. - 148 Bde and 1. Section moved with column under orders of 19. DTR. Hdq. Bde and 2. Sects moved into position under orders of 49. DTR. Wagon lines at RENINGHELST and FLETREN respectively.	
			Hdq DTR located at L. 35. a. 8. 5. Sheet 27	
L. 35. d. 8.5	22.4.18		No. 1. Section under orders of 9. DTR & No 2 Section under orders of 25. DTR	

T2134. Wt. W708—776. 500000. 4/15. Sir J. C. & S.

Army Form C. 2118.

WAR DIARY
or
INTELLIGENCE SUMMARY.
(Erase heading not required.)

3rd Shoot
30 D.T.C.
for April 1918

Instructions regarding War Diaries and Intelligence Summaries are contained in F. S. Regs., Part II. and the Staff Manual respectively. Title pages will be prepared in manuscript.

Place	Date	Hour	Summary of Events and Information	Remarks and references to Appendices
L.35.D.8.5. Sheet 27.	22.4.18		No 1 Section located at L.35.a.7.9 and 2 Section at L.35.b.0.4. No 2 Section under orders HQ D.T.C.	
	24.4.18		Wagon Lines of No 1 Section bombed by E.A. & famous Artillery Wounded.	
	25.4.18		Orders to locate. Shelling HQ moved to L.29.b.6.2. No 1 Section to L.11.c Sheet 27 & No 2 Section to G.11.c.5.1. Sheet 28. - HQ moved again to L.14.b.2.5. Sheet 27.	
L.14.b.2.5.	26.4.18		3 Officers + 30. OR & others to battery to replace casualties. 2nd Lt S.J. Smith E.D. Hall + H. Burkhart wounded.	
	28.4.18		Captain H.C. Allfrey posted from 147 Army Bde 33rd Bde to command the Column on promotion. Lt Magnus - was N.C.O. from Sgt. Stanley to Bdy/Lieut. Sgt. No 107926 Dr T.J. Carter wounded and 5 horses killed belonging to No 1 Section. No 103396. Dr C. Paget and No H/13973 Dr J. Geary wounded and 2 horses killed.	
	29.4.18		No 2 Section moved to L.11.c.3.5. Sheet 27.	
	30.4.18		2 Lts C. Hibbert + S.M. Dile joined from 2nd Bde R.F.A. to join to No 1 Section. Lts V.T. Underwood, E.H. Broad and E.N. Spears joined from Base.	

1.5.18

W.A. Ayres
Major R.F.A.
Commanding 30 D.T.C. R.F.A.

WAR DIARY or INTELLIGENCE SUMMARY

Army Form C. 2118.

30. DAC for May 1918

No. 30

Place	Date	Hour	Summary of Events and Information	Remarks and references to Appendices
L.14.c.2.5 Sheet 27	2.5.18		No. 20762 Sgt H.B. WHITE No.1 Section 30 A.P.C. awarded the French CROIX-DE-GUERRE for gallantry	
	6.5.18		H.Q. DAC & No.1 Section moved to be under orders of 9th DAC & marched Q.13.6.47 Sheet 27 via ABEELE – STEENVOORDE – EECKE. No.1 Section located at Q.19.a.3.3. 4473 at Q.13.b.4.7. H.R.P. at Q.19.b.8.5. Taken over from 25 DAC under orders of 1st Australian DA.	
Q.13.6.47	8.5.18		No.2 Section came to M under orders of H.Q. DAC & marched under orders of 30 DAC to U.13.d.27 from POPERINGHE AHA.	
	10.5.18		No.2 Section relieved the 6th Bde at Q.25.a.3.9 & transmits for ammunition supply from 14pm	
	13.5.18		SAA Section moved from LEDERZEELE to B.6.C.13	
	17.5.18		SAA Section detached under other orders from 30 Division A/7473 of 16.5.18. 2 officers 150 OR 419 Horses & Mules attached into units of 30 Armoured Artillery. Captain F. Cooke goes to No.2 Section in exchange with Captain C Sutherland. Detailed Ranks and equipment handed in to 30/8/8 1st Australian Division who in taking them & Base after having found requirements – Captain C. Sutherland 2 A C Sgts & 70 mules Section transport disbanded	
	21.5.18 6.2am		H.Q. No 1 & 2 Section relieved in the 7 A.D.C.	
	27.5.18 7am		H.Q. No 1 & 2 Section marched to R.K. Q.14.9 per W.W.W. 5 SYLVESTER CAPPEL	

Army Form C. 2118.

WAR DIARY
or
INTELLIGENCE SUMMARY.
(Erase heading not required.)

Sheet 2

30 Mtr
for May 1918

Place	Date	Hour	Summary of Events and Information	Remarks and references to Appendices
			- HAZEBROUCK ROAD to V.5.C.5.1 - EBBLINGHEM to T.22.b.9.4 along road running S.H. through T.28.a and T.27.d. across CANAL-de-NEUF-FOSSE to Ecampenin B.13.a. Struk 26.a to occupied Camp at B.19.a.5.6. 1st June 1918	A.C. Mhpins - Major RE Cmdy 30 Mtr.

Army Form C. 2118.

WAR DIARY
or
INTELLIGENCE SUMMARY.

(Erase heading not required.)

Instructions regarding War Diaries and Intelligence Summaries are contained in F. S. Regs., Part II. and the Staff Manual respectively. Title pages will be prepared in manuscript.

"O.3o. M.T.C"
1x Shut
fr June 1918
Vol 31

Place	Date	Hour	Summary of Events and Information	Remarks and references to Appendices
ROQUINGHEM B.19.a.5.4 Sheet 30 a	15.6.18		There are indications that enemy intends to attack on Corps front at an early date - Ih 30 A.A. started to move to Area "C" West of SERCUS of Column touched via 'ROQUINGHEM - ROAD JUNCTION H3.5.7.9 - BLARINGHEN - X ROADS B.23.6.3.3 - ROAD JUNCTION C.13.6.6.2 - ROAD JUNCTION C.13.6.0.7 and arrived in field at C.8.d.5.5	
SERCUS C.8.d.5.5	17.6.18		In view of shortage of horses - Ammunition Wagon teams reduced from 6 to 4 horses - drivers of these Ammunition Wagons reduced from 3 to 2. - Spare horses in Nos 1 & 2 Sections increased from 40 to 54 - drivers for spare horses in these Sections increased from 20 to 32. - Thus reduction in establishment has been	
		6 pm	effect from 17 June 1918 (Army SAAB WPS 0.13/18/L/S M.12.6.18)	
			No 2. Section moved into billets under 29 H LMA attached to D.S.A. 95.98 - A R.P. at C.12.a.2.2.	
"	20.6.18		Army L.D. Bde Hay withdrawn from this Army. No 2 Section relieved to camp at C.8.d.5-5.	
"	23.6.18		18 Swedish drivers, 17 Snys, L D horses & 9 mules L D Mules consequent on relief of Swedish Sent to WS 2 3rd Armies Remount Depot. A surplus drivers sent to SV Corps Reinforcement for despatch to 2nd Armee R.A. Reinforcement camps	
"			No 1 Section (less drivers) into billets under 1 Sgt A A Attached to D.S.A. 95-98.	

M Anyfrey
Major RFA
Commdy 30 AA Coy.
1st July 1918.

Army Form C. 2118.

WAR DIARY
or
INTELLIGENCE SUMMARY
(Erase heading not required.)

1st Sheet   3. A.T.C.   July 1918

JW 32

Place	Date	Hour	Summary of Events and Information	Remarks and references to Appendices
SERCUS	1.7.18		No 1 Section working from return hut tempored in this wagon room at D.8.c.1 at 9.8.	
	2.7.18		33rd Divisional billeting party (actually under orders of 1st Army Corps – Columns moved from SERCUS via HALLON-CAPPEL – ARNEGHEM to SEMNIRE-CAPPEL No 1 Section harrowed at P.13.c.8.6. and Hg & No 2 Sections at P.14.c.8.0. Sheet 27.	
P.14.c.8.6 Sheet 27	8.7.18		Suddenly under orders of "Brunet X" Corps into reserve. 16th French Corps – at J.G. DONNELLY R.M. adds onto Corps Railway Officer LA CLOCHE.	
	9.7.18		S.A.A. cells on wheels were re-formed at the Army Reinforcement Camp on 22.10.18 regulated at ABBEVILLE on 26.6.18 joined the Advanced Artillery Lorry under orders from 3rd Division and landed at ~D.13.c.8.6.	
	14.7.18		3rd Army in A.R.P. withdrawn at P.24.c.4.8. – 2nd & Gold. L. PZE. Admd officer in charge.	
	28.7.18		A.R.P. at P.20.a.4.8. handed over to 29 Armoured Artillery and came to A.R.V. established at P.12.b.8.9. Ammunition brought to the dump by Light Railway.	
	29.7.18		Column moved from Louvan Dump to STEENVOORDE Area – Hq located at P.6.C.5.8. No 1 Section P.6.C.2.6. – No 2 Section P.6.C.6.2. Sqd. Section P.6.C.5.8.	
P.6.C.8.6	29.7.18		G.O.C. 3rd Division inspected the Column – Drill order – mounted.	
	30.7.18		13 Hosky Wagon + 78 G.S.Wagons + 18 Section engaged in taking 1600 rds.	

Army Form C. 2118.

WAR DIARY
or
INTELLIGENCE SUMMARY.
(Erase heading not required.)

2o Sheet   3o D.A.C   for July 1918

Place	Date	Hour	Summary of Events and Information	Remarks and references to Appendices
P.L.C.S.B. Sheet 57	31/7/18		A + A+ and 10TG rds B+ for forward Gun positions - No 1187909 Dr. T. Ball killed, also 4 multi Rods and 2 wounded, in No 1. Section. No Casualties in No 2 Section. Montague Ammunition Dump taken over from the 39th Division by 2nd Rd-sect 31/4. Owing to 149 Bde. 41.18ph Bty 148 Bde being detailed to take the place of 77 HF.A.Bde for local protection to in Corps, not by 35th Division. No 1 + 2 Sections instructed to support 149 Bde in getting their ammunition up to the Gun Position.	

W Aufrere -
Major RA
Comdg 3o D.A.C

18/18.

Army Form C. 2118.

WAR DIARY
or
INTELLIGENCE SUMMARY.

(Erase heading not required.)

30 D.P.C.

J. Split

for August 1918

33

Place	Date	Hour	Summary of Events and Information	Remarks and references to Appendices
P.6.C.8.8 (Sheet 7)	12.8.18		The 30 Aus Hty Battery 35 Siege and Batteries on the lines. As usual withdrawn in Communication Supply Train to Jnr. – DAMASCI — VINTAGE Emmaneline Supply train to 35 D.P.C. the A.T.R. at R.I.A.11.5 (Sheet 7) Taken over from 35 D.P.C. Sections to remain in their present lines.	
	17.8		No 1 & 2 Sections have on present now taking Ammunition to Gun positions	
			16 Cd. Dragoons attaches to the 2nd A.L.H. Bde for Convoy & mustered to the lines	
	23.8.18		3 N.U. C.D.S. French Cavalry Scout attachment 1 mule B.I. and Soldier to Squadron	
			Enemy Bns. Uy no hostilities on frontage	
	25.8.18		6 Indian & 4 Haganis engaged nightly until 3rd inst in Convoying for brigades in 4 Bernal Coy. B.B. to the line	
	26.8.18		Hagan Lewis occupied by the detachment attached to 30. But to the B.B. Sheet at 11.30 pm 1 Mule killed, 1 mule & 2 horses wounded. Detachment turned to find lines at Q.17.b.8.4	
	31.8.18		S.A.A. Section taken over by Divisional "Q" or ordered to move at 2 am Red Guard or NOT NOT Section received orders to move and left camp at 4 am arriving at Divisional SHARP at 6 am Headquarters at B.2.b.3.6	

A.C. [signature] 1.9.18
Major
Commanding 30th D.P.C.

Army Form C. 2118.

WAR DIARY
or
INTELLIGENCE SUMMARY.
(Erase heading not required.)

Vol 34

30.9.18
for September 1918

Place	Date	Hour	Summary of Events and Information	Remarks and references to Appendices
R.7.6.3.6. Sheet 27	1.9.18		HQ Nos 1 + 2 Sections moved from GODEWAERSVELDE Area to HESTOUTRE Area and located as follows:- HQ M.2.a.1.1. No 1 Section M.2.a.1.1. No 2 Section N.1.d.3.0. Sheet 28. Signal Section remaining at R.1.C. Sheet 27. 30.1 A.S.P. established at N.3.C.3.1 Sheet 28 under 2/Lt H. IRVINE.	
N.2.a.1.1. Sheet 28	15.9.18		Party sent to collect remounts at Calais.	
	19.9.18		2/Lt D. Pike and party of men sent to take over the 30.1 A.S.P at S.3.d.2.7.	
	20.9.18		Column moved to CROIX-de-POPERINGHE area by Henry location HQ M.36.C.8.6. No 1 Section M.33.C.35.15. No 2 Section M.32.6.6.6. San Section M.32.6.70.45. Forward Ammunition Dumps under 2nd D. Pile established at LINDENHOEK cct.	
Croix de POPERINGHE	29.9.18		1000 Nos A 500 AR and 1000 BX.	
	30.9.18		During the month the two Sections Salvo from old arenas fire trenches Enemy went on enemy retirement 24338 rounds 18pr and 8190 rounds of 4.5. 30.1 A.S.P. issued (Serviceable) and 2000 RDs. 18pr and 1845 rounds 4.5 howty. (Serviceable Ammunition).	

1.10.18

[signatures]
Lieut 30 Div DAC
Capt 30 Div DAC

Army Form C. 2118.

WAR DIARY or INTELLIGENCE SUMMARY.

(Erase heading not required.)

I Shot

30 Oct.

for October 1918

WO 3 [?]

Instructions regarding War Diaries and Intelligence Summaries are contained in F. S. Regs., Part II. and the Staff Manual respectively. Title pages will be prepared in manuscript.

Place	Date	Hour	Summary of Events and Information	Remarks and references to Appendices
Shot 28				
CROIX du [?]	1.10.18		H.Q. No 1 & 2 Sections moved to LINDENHOEK - WYTSCHAETE - Roads and located in N.28.a.9.9. Spare Sections moved under orders of Division O. and locals at HULVERGHEM - Rd.d. at LINDENHOEK	
POPERINGHE				
N.28.d.9.9.	2.10.18		Convoy of Ammunition from No.1 Section firing to gun positions of 9"/4.8. Shells at MESSINES - Dvr J. Scullion Killed. Dvr T. Wilson and Dvr R. Wilkins wounded. 3 horses killed and 2 wounded.	
" "	3.10.18		Convoy of Ammunition from H.Q. firing lines of 9"/4.8. from No.1 Section. Shells on HULVERGHEM - MESSINES Road. Dvr R. Byrth wounded and 2 horses killed.	
" "	7.10.18		A.R.P. moved from LINDENHOEK to KEMMEL Church.	
" "	16.10.18		H.Q. No.1 & 2 Sections moved to St ELOI via VIERSTRAAT KRUISSTRAATHOEK - VOORMEZEELE to Wagon lines No 32.C.5.4. M.R.P. established at St Eloi. Spare Section moved under orders of Division O.	
I.32.C.5.4.	17.10.18		Ammunition Supply well in hand. F.A.T. Chaplin i/c for the barrage. No ammunition in regard if first convoy in "still" Echelons to be mandated - motor Cyclist attached for inter-communication between MRP and M.T. Echelon.	
" "	18.10.18		H.Q. moved via HOLLEBEKE - ZANDEVOORDE - TENBRIELEN to Wagon lines at OOGHEET FARM D.13.A.1.4. No 1 & 2 Sections attached to 14.8 and 109 Bdes. respectively (Ginchmore group and Shootmagroup) moved under the orders of Bde. Commanders. No.1 Section on HOLLEBEKE - ZANDEVOORDE - GHELUVELT	

Army Form C. 2118.

2. Sheet

WAR DIARY
or
INTELLIGENCE SUMMARY.
(Erase heading not required.)

Instructions regarding War Diaries and Intelligence Summaries are contained in F. S. Regs., Part II. and the Staff Manual respectively. Title pages will be prepared in manuscript.

Place	Date	Hour	Summary of Events and Information	Remarks and references to Appendices
			Crossing the River LYS. H. portion at BOUSBECQUE to trafic lines in the Racing Track at HALLUIN	
			No 2 Section marched to H.5. Central Sheet 28	
OOGHEET. FM	19.10.18		HQ OPC moved to RONCQ. No 1 Section to N.31.a.9.8. Sheet 9. No 2 Section to J.1.6.9.9 sheet 29.	
STERHOEK	20.10.18		HQ moved to STERHOEK S.H.6.8 + Sheet 29. CROISE BREAK. No 1 Section to ROLLEGHEM.	
	21.10.18		No 2. Section moved to N. 31. a.	
STERHOEK	22.10.18		HQ moved to COYGHEM. No 1. Section to T. 17. a. No 2. Section T. 11. C.	
COYGHEM	24.10.18		Portion of A + B Smoke Ammunition both Carried by lorri. 1 armd lorrie to 3 ordinary lorries	
"	26.10.18		Arrisson crew to refit for transfer on M.T. Coy - Motor Cyclist returnd to M.T. Coy - Indents	
			for Ammunition to be submitted to corps G.	
			Searchlights returned dept. and posted at T. 16. b.	
"	30.10.18		1000 rds + 3 Smoke debris from province of 07/145 + 07/149 respectively.	
			Indian Personnel. (150. 0.R) from Lumun from RUEN.	
	31.10.18		HQ OPC moved to ROLLEGHEM.	

Olurn
Capt. R.D.
for OC 30 DAC

1.11.18

T2134. Wt. W708—776. 500000. 4/15. Sir J. C. & S.

Army Form C. 2118.

WAR DIARY
or
INTELLIGENCE SUMMARY.

(Erase heading not required.)

3rd Sqdn.
for N/November 1918.

Place	Date	Hour	Summary of Events and Information	Remarks and references to Appendices
Sheet 29.				
POLLEGHEM	4.XI.18		No. 1 & 2 Sections moved from T.16 & 17 to O.14 a 5.5 Sheet 29. Ammunition Refilling Point established at O.14 c.7.7. Ammunition taken over from 1st Division Ammunition at T.18 c. (approx)	
	5.XI.18		Sg. Sg. Magmo to ground R.A.P. at O.14 c.7.7 Shooting. SAA Section moved to O.13 d.1.9 Shooting	
	6.XI.18		HQ A.C.C. moved to BELLEGHEM. Lieut J.H. HOUDE A.V.C. joined and took Norwich to Barili Sect.	
BELLEGHEM	9.XI.18		HQ A.C.C. moved to O.14 a.5.5	
O.14 a.5.5 Sheet 29	10.XI.18		Nos. 1 & 2 Section at SPA Section moved to AVELGHEM. Ammunition Refilling Point at Factory AVELGHEM	
AVELGHEM	11.XI.18		ARMISTICE in force 11.00 hours. No. 1 & 2 Sections Commenced clearing all Ammunition from four positions to R.R.P. AVELGHEM	
	12.XI.18		All Sg. Magmo turned in to Corps A.S.C. with Supplies.	
	19.XI.18		On clearing of all gun positions of Ammunition in charge of 30 A.A. 36 A.A. + 38th Divns. completed today. Column moved from AVELGHEM La Pilletto at RUDDERVOORDE and PETIT TOURCOING. Guards left in charge	
	23.XI.18		of Ammunition on Dumps at O.14 c.7.7 and Factory R.I.80.54 under orders from 19th Corps. Guards left at Dumps O.14 b. Factory AVELGHEM unknown	
RUDDERVOORDE	29.XI.18			

1.XII.18

Army Form C. 2118.

WAR DIARY
or
INTELLIGENCE SUMMARY.
(Erase heading not required.)

30th D.A.C. R.F.A.
DECEMBER

Instructions regarding War Diaries and Intelligence Summaries are contained in F.S. Regs., Part II. and the Staff Manual respectively. Title pages will be prepared in manuscript.

Place	Date	Hour	Summary of Events and Information	Remarks and references to Appendices
Ruddervoorde	2/12/18		Proceeded by "Route march" to Nevirghem & stayed there on the night of 2/3 December 1918.	
Nevirghem	3/12/18		March continued, to Thienen nr Ammentien.	
Thienen	11/12/18		First draft of Cadremen left D.A.C. for England on Demobilization.	Adjutant hurt RPM Adj. 30 DAC

9/11 37

T2134. Wt. W708—776. 500000. 4/15. Sir J. C. & S.

www.ingramcontent.com/pod-product-compliance
Lightning Source LLC
Chambersburg PA
CBHW081425160426
43193CB00013B/2196